Annotated Text Copyright © 2025 Josh W. Slatten.
Published by Billy the Kid's Historical Coalition.

Cover design by Pierre Delacôte.

While the text of John W. Poe's *The Death of Billy the Kid* is now in public domain, the new annotated text and added chapters are copyright of the author. All rights reserved. No part of this publication may be reproduced, distributed, or transmitted in any form or by any means, including photocopying, recording, or other electronic or mechanical methods, without the prior written permission of the publisher, except in the case of brief quotations embodied in critical reviews and certain other noncommercial uses permitted by copyright law.

THE DEATH OF BILLY THE KID

By John Poe

Annotated by Josh W. Slatten

The Wild West has always called to me- a place of grit, legends and untold stories. But this is more than a story; it's a window into the life of Billy the Kid and the people that shaped him. With this annotated edition, we bring Poe's words to life, adding context and depth to his firsthand account.
This book is a labor of love—a testament to our commitment to keeping the spirit of The Kid alive. This is dedicated the many supporters and followers of The Coalition. Thank you for helping us save history.

"He covered me with his six-shooter as quick as lightning."

Illustration from the December 1919 issue of *Wide World Magazine* of the Kid coming across Poe.

Contents

Author's Note	9
The Fulton Introduction	11
The Death of Billy the Kid	39
The Hunt	51
Reconnoitering Fort Sumner	69
Strange Sequence of Happenings the Night of July 14, 1881	81
Inquest and Burial	107
The Final Moments of Billy the Kid	
A Pictorial Essay	121
The Death of John W. Poe	129
Epilogue	133
Index	135
About the Author	139

Author's Note

During the research for this project, my intention was to provide readers with the most comprehensive account of the events surrounding the death of Billy the Kid. I focused particularly on the firsthand account given by Deputy John William Poe. While I do not claim that all mentioned accounts are correct, I believe it is important to bring them to light and allow readers to form their own opinions based on the most complete information ever presented in print. When quoting newspaper accounts and various interviews, I have preserved the contents in their original form, refraining from correcting grammatical errors and punctuation. This approach aims to allow readers to experience the most authentic feel for the material presented.

In the following pages, you will encounter the story of Billy the Kid's death as recounted by John Poe. This account was initially published in the December 1919 issue of *Wild World Magazine* before becoming its own standalone book in 1933. Accompanying this story is Maurice Fulton's introduction from the 1933 release, presented in its original form. Unlike many contemporary accounts of the Kid's life, Fulton's rendition has aged quite well and still stands as a true and accurate testimony of Billy the Kid's life.

I hope you enjoy the research presented here, and more importantly, I hope it pays tribute to John William Poe and the fascinating life he led, which has been overlooked by many until now.

John William Poe, ca.1879. *Courtesy of the Historical Society for Southeast New Mexico.*

The Fulton Introduction

In a straightforward, plain, and mater-of-fact style that adds sincerity to the recital, the late John W. Poe has recorded fully the circumstances of the death of Billy the Kid. His knowledge was first-hand, for he was one of the posse of three who, in the midsummer of 1881, very unexpectedly, both to themselves and everyone else, gave New Mexico and the Texas Panhandle everlasting riddance from the young scapegrace. Though the account was not written until nearly thirty-five years later, Mr. Poe's undimmed memory and love of exact statement make the narrative fully as trustworthy as if written immediately after the event.

To one like myself, who saw Mr. Poe but casually in the tranquility of 1922-23, the last year of his somewhat more than threescore and ten, there was little to suggest how largely the earlier half of his life had been filled with frontier hardships and dangers. The large, broad-shouldered physique, together with an impressive gravity of demeanor, betokened that the man sitting at the president's desk of the Citizens' National Bank of Roswell, New Mexico, was a person of consequence, possibly of great courage and determination, but did not give the passer-by an inkling of the roles he had played in ushering in law and order upon the raw and raucous Southwestern frontier.

John Poe and EA Cahoon sitting at his desk at the First Bank of Roswell, ca. 1895. *Courtesy of the Historical Society for Southeast New Mexico.*

At the urge of an adventurous spirit, Mr. Poe had left his boyhood home on a Kentucky farm at seventeen, and 'gone West.' By the spring of 1871 he had penetrated Kansas and was then at the end of the Santa Fe Railroad, then slightly below Emporia, making a livelihood as a member of a construction crew. In 1872, he was a step farther into the unsettled parts, cutting timber and crossties on Red River in Texas and the Indian Territory. In the spring of 1872, he pulled up stakes and traveled horseback two hundred and fifty miles farther west of Fort Griffin, then almost the *ultima thule* of the frontier. Here he handled a large wood contract for the garrison, but when this was completed, he became one of the crowd of buffalo-hunters who were swarming over the plains of West Texas. In the four years (1874-1878) spent on the buffalo range, Mr. Poe made a reputation as one of the most successful hunters. His estimate that he had killed in the neighborhood of twenty thousand buffalo with his own Sharps suggests both his skill and the lucrativeness of the business.

The old Fort Griffin Jail.
Courtesy of the Library of Congress.

When buffalo-hunting ceased to be profitable, Mr. Poe entered upon several years of service as law-enforcement officer by accepting appointment as town marshal for Fort Griffin. In his capacity he served but one year, long enough, however, to show his remarkable qualifications. He held a tight rein on that very rough and cosmopolite town without killing a single person. Such a record won him higher recognition in 1879, when he became a Deputy United States Marshal. He was at once stationed at Fort Elliott in the northeast corner of the Texas Panhandle, then in the throes of the bold, reckless life incident to its first settlement. Cattle-stealing was rampant, but Mr. Poe curbed it so markedly that the Canadian River Cattlemen's Association selected him to look especially after their interests. How this employment led to a special mission into New Mexico, Mr. Poe relates at the beginning of is story.

Fort Elliott in 1881. *Courtesy of the Library of Congress.*

It will clarify matters somewhat, however, if we understand how Billy the Kid, the particular thorn in the flesh of the Panhandle cattlemen whom Mr. Poe was commissioned to remove, had developed. The limits of an introduction forbid a full-length account of William Bonney, *alias* William Antrim (to give the equipment of names under which he usually appears in legal documents) who has nowadays become simply Billy the Kid. We cannot take space even to divest the first states of his career of the legendizing that unquestionably envelops them; nor can we chronicle his part in the feud known as the Lincoln County War. Suffice it to say that when those disorders almost ceased in the summer of 1878, he had taken a prominent part in all the fighting and emerged with a reputation for coolness and shooting skill that was remarkable for one just leaving behind his teens. But the hand of the law was clutching at him with two indictments - one for the killing of Sheriff William Brady, the other for the killing of his deputy, George Hindman, an outrageous deed which Billy the Kid and five or six others of his clique had accomplished on April 1, 1878.

A rare image showing the back of the Tunstall store and what was once the corral that concealed the Regulators on the morning of April 1, 1878. Photo ca. 1950.

The defeated remnant of the McSween faction, including Billy the Kid, withdrew to Fort Sumner, about ninety miles northeast of Lincoln. This old army establishment was now shorn of the prestige it had possessed ten years before, when the Bosque Redondo experiment was in progress, seeking to impound and civilize the several thousand Navajos and Mescalero Apaches on the large reservation established on the Rio Pecos. The remains of the fort, including several square miles of land and a collection of buildings originally built by the United States Government for officers' quarters, barracks, storehouses, stables, and outhouses, had been purchased by Lucien B. Maxwell, of Maxwell Land Grant fame, who, after the loss of his vast estate on the Cimarron, had moved into the southern part of the Territory in an effort to recoup his fortune. In the course of time, Lucien B. Maxwell had been gathered to his fathers, but his son Pedro, more commonly called Pete, had succeeded to the headship of the family and the management of the sheep and cattle interests.

Fort Sumner Military post, ca.1868. The main building in this image served as the Infantry Quarters. The building in the far background, almost out of view, is the (then) Indian hospital where Tom Folliard was killed.

During the sojourn at Fort Sumner, Billy the Kid came into friendship with the Maxwell's. The Family seems to have been largely feminine, and Billy the Kid's personality and career had elements which made him attractive to that sex. Mrs. Maxwell, her daughters, and even the Navajo servant-woman, Deluvina, grew attached to him, and welcomed his presence whenever

The Death of Billy the Kid: Annotated Edition

he was near Fort Sumner. It is still a moot question whether there developed between the young outlaw and one of the Maxwell daughters any more lively degree of interest than friendly acquaintance, but the present writer himself discounts heavily the echoes of the old gossip that may still be heard or found in print.

During the late summer and early fall of 1878, Lincoln County was in perhaps a worse state than when the Lincoln County War was in active progress. Instead of simply two warring factions, several bands of outlaws where roaming at will and harrying the land and its inhabitants. During all this pell-mell havoc and confusion, Billy the Kid began to emerge more and more as what, in present-day parlance, would be called a 'public enemy,' He came back into Lincoln on several occasions, accompanied by some of his former McSween adherents, and stole horses, which they carried into the Panhandle to sell. On one such foray, the clerk at the Indian Agency, Bernstein, was killed, and while Billy the Kid was not actually responsible, yet it was generally ascribed to him and became the basis for issuing a United States warrant for him.

In October the new governor, General Lew Wallace, came to New Mexico, clothed with plenipotentiary power to quiet the disorders. His program at first was all for mild measures. So far as old offenders were concerned, he would wipe the slate clean at once. In November he issued an amnesty proclamation extending a general pardon to both factions for what had been done between February and November 1878, but with the proviso that the terms of this offer might not be taken advantage of by 'any person in bar of conviction under indictment now found and returned for any such crimes and misdemeanors.' This limitation shut the door upon the Kid, under a double indictment for the killing of Brady and Hindman. He probably was not highly uncomfortable under the situation, for the officers of the law had virtually given over their attempts to arrest him. The fall term of court had been pretermitted, and this created a lapse of several months before there would be any activity on the part of those charged with arresting offenders or dispensing justice.

Lew Wallace at age 50, as he appeared when meeting with Billy the Kid.

By February 1879, the two original factions were ready to patch up a peace, and a conference was held in Lincoln. Billy the Kid, Tom O'Folliard, and probably one of the Salazars, representing the former McSween group, and Jesse Evans, Tom Campbell and James J. Dolan, representing the former Murphy-Dolan-Riley contingent, met and drew up terms of peace. But hardly was the ink dry on the document when the feud flared up again. As the conferees and several of their friends were going down the street of Lincoln celebrating the newly established era of amity and good-will, they encountered Huston J. Chapman, a lawyer of the trouble-making type whom Mrs. McSween had secured to look after her interests. For three or four months he had been a veritable gadfly both to the Dolan faction and to the military at Fort Stanton, especially Colonel Nathan A. M. Dudley, the commanding officer, who had come to the rescue of the Dolan crowd when they were hard pressed towards the end of the five-day battle at Lincoln in July. There was a clash of words between the Dolan group and Chapman, followed by two shots which left the lawyers body lifeless on the streets. If the old indictments mean anything, Campbell and Dolan were considered the principals in the killing, while Jesse Evans was an accessory.

Colonel Nathan Dudley, standing portrait taken in Baton Rouge c.1863. *Wikipedia.*

A diagram of the Chapman killing. *Illustration by Larry Gosser.*

Governor Wallace felt that the Chapman killing indicated a new and possibly more serious outbreak than before. He came upon the scene and took personal charge of the arrest of those responsible for the murder. One of the first his mind turned toward was Billy the Kid, and the letter to Colonel Edward Hatch, then commanding the troops in New Mexico, was short and pointed:

I have just ascertained that the Kid is at a place called Las Tablas, a plazita up near Coghlin's ranch. He has with him Thomas O'Folliard, and was going out of the Territory, but stopped there to rest his horses, saying he would stop a few days. He was at the house of one Salazar.

You will oblige me by sending a detachment after the two men; and if they are caught, send them on to Fort Stanton for trial as accessories to the murder of Chapman.

Squire Wilson's home where Billy met the governor.
Illustration by Larry Gosser.

Greathouse Station and Tavern. *Illustration by Larry Gosser*

James Carlyle's headstone. The headstone was placed in August, 2022 by Billy the Kid's Historical Coalition.

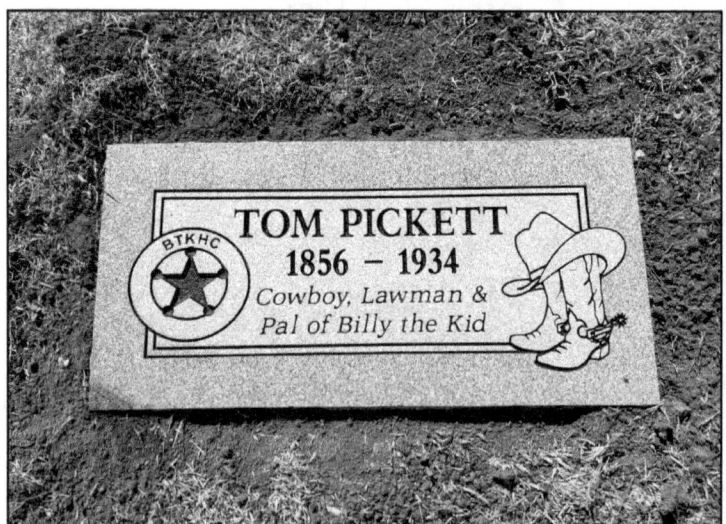

Tom Pickett's headstone in the Desert View Cemetery, in Winslow, Arizona. This marker was placed in April, 2023 by Billy the Kid's Historical Coalition.

Brazil and Wilcox Ranch in later years, c.1920.

Brazil and Wilcox Ranch site as it appears today. *Photo taken in 2024.*

Early day view of courthouse.

A view similar to what the Kid would have seen when standing on the courthouse balcony, just after killing Bell and Olinger. Unk. date

THE DEATH OF BILLY THE KID: ANNOTATED EDITION

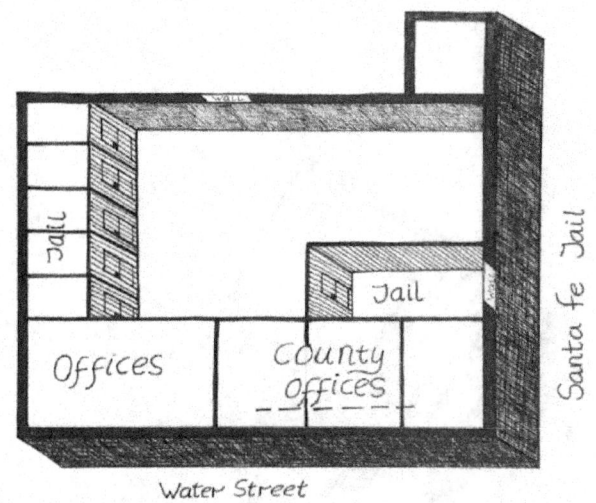

The Santa Fe jail. Detailed from the 1883 Santa Fe Sanborn Fire Insurance Map. *Illustration by Mel Hubner.*

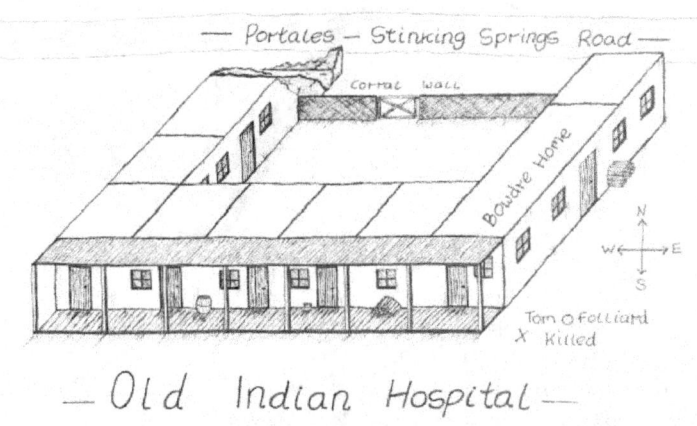

The old Indian Hospital. *Illustration by Mel Hubner.*

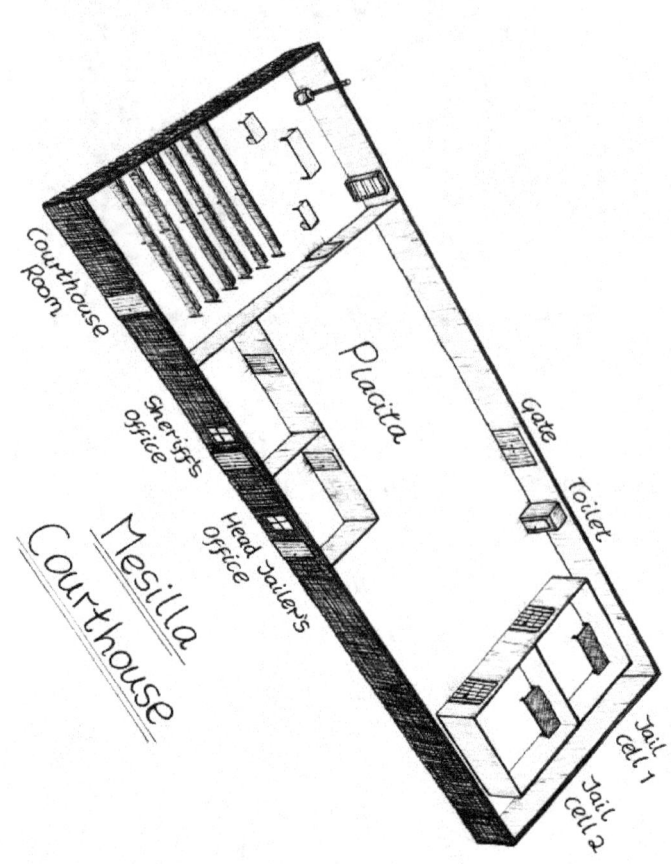

Courthouse diagram. This diagram is based on the independent research of historian David Thomas. For further information, see his book, *The Trial of Billy the Kid*. Illustration courtesy of Mel Hubner.

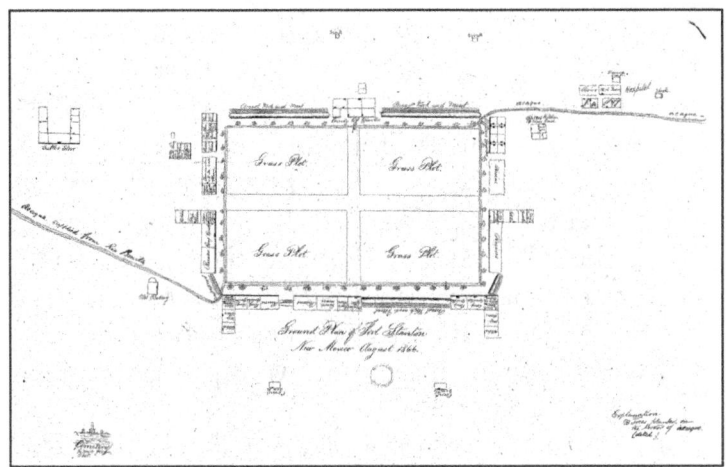

Ground plan of Fort Stanton, August 1866. *Illustration courtesy of Larry Walker.*

If the men found to have left Las Tablas, I beg them may be pursued until caught. The details are commended to your good judgment.

News of the Governor's determination must have reached Billy the Kid, for, as the following letter to Governor Wallace, written a few days later, shows, he sought to bespeak for himself some sort of special dispensation:

> I have heard that you will give one thousand ($) for my body, which as I can understand it means alive as a witness. I know it is as a witness against those that murdered Mr. Chapman. If it was so as I could appear at court, I could give the desired information, but I have indictments against me for things that happened in the Lincoln County War and am afraid to give myself up because my enemies would kill me. The day Mr. Chapman was murdered, I was in Lincoln at the request of good citizens to meet Mr. J.J. Dolan, to meet as a friend

so as to be able to lay aside our arms and go to work. I was present when Mr. Chapman was murdered and know who did it; and if it were not for those indictments, I would have made it clear before now. If it is in your power to annul those indictments, I hope you will do so, so as to give me a chance to explain. Please send me an answer telling me what you can do. You can send answer by bearer. I have no wish to fight anymore; indeed, I have not raised an arm since your proclamation. As to my character I refer you to any of the citizens, for the majority of them are my friends and have been helping me all they could. I am called Kid Antrim, but Antrim is my stepfather's name.

Waiting an answer I remain,
Your obedient servant
W.H. Bonney

Juan Patron's home and store, ca. 1926.

The Death of Billy the Kid: Annotated Edition

Negotiations, both by letters and by interview, finally brought the Governor and the young outlaw into an understanding by which Billy the Kid was to undergo pseudo-arrest by Sheriff Kimbrell. The program was carried out, and Billy the Kid lodged under guard in the Patron Store building in Lincoln, pending the approaching session of the grand jury. When court convened about the middle of April, he was one of the witnesses whose testimony resulted in the indictment of Dolan, Campbell, and Jesse Evans in connection with the Chapman killing. The Kid himself appeared in court and pleaded not guilty to the indictments against him for the Brady-Hindman killing. A change of venue to Dona Ana County was allowed, an arrangement which postponed his trial a month or two.

BILLY THE KID.

$500 REWARD.

I will pay $500 reward to any person or persons who will capture William Bonny, alias The Kid, and deliver him to any sheriff of New Mexico. Satisfactory proofs of identity will be required.

LEW. WALLACE,
Governor of New Mexico.

This notice ran in the Las Vegas Gazette from December 13, 1880 until Billy the Kid's capture on December 23. This same notice then ran through May of 1881 in the Santa Fe New Mexican, after the Kid's jailbreak.

In the interval, however, Billy the Kid suffered a change of heart. Just before time to be taken over to La Mesilla for trial, he escaped and took refuge at Fort

Sumner. Why he did this is hard to determine now. Possibly with faith weakened regarding Governor Wallace's ability to guarantee immunity, especially when the district judge, Warren Bristol, and the district attorney, William L. Rynerson, were implacably hostile to the McSween faction as well as politically opposed to Governor Wallace. Probably he also realized that if he did happen to 'come clear' at the trial, he would face the enmity of the Dolan faction, embittered by his testimony before the grand jury. At any rate, he elected to burn his bridges behind him, and at once resumed his former habit of looking out for himself with the aid of his trusty firearms.

Billy the Kid's Cave, ca. 1905.

He was at large in the vicinity of Fort Sumner for approximately a year and a half. The question of a livelihood he met through monte dealing and cattle-stealing. At the point of the pistol, he had presented a claim to John S. Chisum for five hundred dollars back pay for services rendered during the Lincoln County

War, but the wily old cattle baron denied the claim, and out-argued the Kid into lowering the revolver. The Kid, however, bestowed a parting threat that he would obtain the five hundred dollars in good measure from the Chisum herds, and he and his companions proceeded to make good the threat. Their cattle-stealing, however, soon passed the reprisal stage, and became a definitely organized business. His gang grew until it included, not only Charlie Bowdre and Tom O'Folliard, but also some even rougher men who had drifted into Fort Sumner, such as Dave Rudabaugh, Tom Pickett, and Billy Wilson. Even the community itself at Fort Sumner probably furnished some recruits.

Frank Stewart in later years.
Photo courtesy of Ancestory.

Fort Sumner was advantageously located as a base for such a business. About forty miles east, in the vicinity of Las Portales Lake, was an ideal hide-out, where the booty might be concealed. It was easy to take horses out into the Panhandle and find a ready market at Tascosa and other settlements. It was equally easy to gather up on the return a bunch of cattle and carry them down through Fort Sumner and into Lincoln County, where Pat Coghlin at Tularosa had a depot ready and waiting for stolen cattle, which to fulfill his government contract. It was such systems that brought to a head the irritation of the Panhandle cattlemen. Frank Stewart, as special agent, came over into New Mexico with a posse in the early part of December 1881, to retake cattle supposedly in the vicinity of Fort Sumner and in the hand of Billy the Kid's gang. But prior to this the toils had begun to close around the Kid. As sheriff-elect of Lincoln County, Pat Garrett had already begun his stern pursuit of the Kid and his followers. The Kid aggravated the case against himself, when in the latter part of November 1880, he killed a popular resident of White Oaks, Jim Carlyle, in a fight at the Greathouse Ranch with a posse from White Oaks. Garrett carried the pursuit shortly afterward strait into Fort Sumner, in the vicinity of which the Kid's gang was hiding. Frank Stewart and his men from the Canadian joined forces with Garrett's posse. O'Folliard was killed by means of ambush; a little later, the Kid, Rudabaugh, Bowdre, Tom Pickett, and Billy Wilson were rounded up in a small hut at Stinking Springs. Bowdre was killed, the hat he was wearing causing him to be mistaken for the Kid. The remaining four decided then on surrender.

Old Home of the notorious Billy The Kid, near Taiban, N. M.
Pub. for J. R. Dumas, Taiban, N. M.

Stinking Springs rock house. It was originally believed that this image was published as a postcard in the 1930's. However, recent research indicates that it was in circulation as early as 1908.

The Death of Billy the Kid: Annotated Edition

The Santa Fe jail, ca. 1895.

The Kid was taken to Santa Fe, where he was kept in jail until April 1881, when he was taken down to La Mesilla for trial. This was quickly over, and the Kid sentenced by Judge Bristol to be hanged on May 13 at Lincoln. His dramatic escape is perhaps too well known to be given here at any greater length than in the words Garrett wrote on the order of execution:

"I certify that I rec'd the within named William Bonney alias Kid alias William Antrim into my custody on the 21st day of April, A.D. 1881. And I further certify that on April 28th the said Wm. Bonney alias Kid alias William Antrim made his escape by killing his guard, J.W. Bell and Robert Olinger in Lincoln, New Mexico."

This exhibition of derring-do put Billy the Kid more on a pedestal than before and attracted toward him the instinctive admiration of all lovers of 'the art of daring,' to use the phrase of Mirabeau. Up to this point in his career, opinion had been divided. Was he a sneaks-by or a lad of mettle, a ruffian or a hero? - and no definite answer seemed possible. But after this escape, popular imagination seized him for its darling and recognized in him more than a common killer and thief, more than a common leech on society. Even the *Santa Fe New Mexican*, always disparaging of the Kid, bestowed a grudging plaudit in the issues of May 4, 1881, a few days after the escape:

The above [the account of Kid's escape] is the record of as bold a deed as those versed in the annals of crime can recall. It surpasses anything of which the Kid had been guilty, so far that his past offenses lose much of heinousness in comparison with it, and it effectually settles the question as to whether the Kid is a cowardly cut-throat or a thoroughly reckless and fearless man. Never before has he faced death boldly or run any great risk in the perpetration of his bloody deeds. Bob Olinger used to say that he was a cur, and that every man he had killed had been murdered in cold blood and without the slightest chance of defending himself. The Kid displayed no disposition to correct this until this last bitter experience that his theory was anything but correct.

Courthouse building, La Mesilla, ca. 1885. It was in this building that the Kid was tried and sentenced to hang.

THE DEATH OF BILLY THE KID: ANNOTATED EDITION

Illustration from the December 1919 issue of *Wide World Magazine* of Poe talking to the locals in Fort Sumner.

But from such an Apollo, the Kid's life turns almost into the commonplace in its last scene. This young outlaw, with a Territorial reward of five hundred dollars upon his head, hides himself in the friendly camp of a Mexican sheepherder and palters with the idea of leaving the country, at least for a time. One July night he seeks the sociability of a *baile* at the home of one of the leading Mexican ranch-owners in the vicinity of Fort Sumner. After the dance ends about eleven o'clock, he rides back to the sheep camp of the Mexican friend with whom he is hiding, and then decides to go over to the Maxwell ranch. About midnight he reaches the room of one of the employees of the Maxwells living in the long row of adobe rooms to the south of the building in which the Maxwell family lived.

John W. Poe and Josh W. Slatten

After divesting himself of shoes and garments superfluous on a July night to a man seeking relaxation, he grows hungry, and, learning that a freshly killed quarter of beef is hanging on the north porch of the Maxwell dwelling, he sallies forth, butcher-knife in hand, and *sans* shoes and shirt, across the intervening yard, to cut for himself a piece of meat. His route takes him past two members of the posse at the end of the south porch, and at this point he seems to lose the genius for preserving his own life by means of his flaming pistol which heretofore had stood him in such good stead. He moves on past the two strangers, who must have been revealed fully to him in the moonlight, and dodges into the doorway of Pete Maxwell's bedroom, there to confront the pistol held by Pat Garrett and from it to receive his *coup de grace*.

John W. Poe standing beside Roswell leader, Captain J.C. Lea. *Courtesy Historical Society for Southeast New Mexico.*

The Death of Billy the Kid: Annotated Edition

It was never easy to draw out Mr. Poe about the death of the Kid, but when he did relate the story, his listeners found it interesting and profitable hearing. At Mrs. Poe's urging, he finally wrote out the account and turned it over to her to keep against whatever time might be suitable for its publication. In the early part of 1919, Mr. Edward Seymour, of New York, a gentleman interested in the history of the West, feeling skeptical about certain information regarding the death of the Kid which had come to him, inquired of the late Charles Goodnight as to a reliable source of information. Mr. Goodnight referred him to Mr. Poe, making the comment that 'whatever John Poe would furnish would be true.' As the easiest way of giving Mr. Seymour the facts, Mr. Poe sent him a copy of the account Mrs. Poe was treasuring. This eventually reached Mr. E.A. Brininstool, of Los Angeles, who perceiving its value, secured its publication in an English magazine, *The Wide World*, for December 1919. Afterward Mr. Brininstool published the account as a privately printed brochure, which in the course of time passed into the limbo of 'out of print.'

The present volume gives to his grim episode of the old Southwest that definitive and permanent form it richly merits, considering its importance as source material.

Maurice Garland Fulton

Maurice Garland Fulton on a visit to Lincoln. *Library of Congress.*

THE DEATH OF BILLY THE KID

The original text of John Poe is followed by the *author's annotations in italic*

The only authenticated image of Billy the Kid. According to Paulita Maxwell Jaramillo in an interview with Walter Noble Burns in the mid 1920's, she told him the photo was taken by a traveling photographer who came through Fort Sumner in late 1879 or early 1880. Paulita was very critical of the only known picture, saying; I never liked the picture, I don't think it does Billy justice. It makes him look rough and uncouth. This image is a first-generation scan of Billy the Kid. *Courtesy of Richard Weddle.*

The Death of Billy the Kid

During the winter of 1880-81 I was living in the Panhandle of Texas, where for some time previous I had been serving as deputy U.S. marshal, and also as deputy sheriff.

> *In the winter of 1880-81, Billy the Kid was held in custody at the Santa Fe jail. He remained there until his transfer to Mesilla for trial on Monday, March 28, 1881. Source: Thomas, David. The Trial of Billy the Kid. Doc45 Publishing, 2021. p. 47.*

About the middle of that winter the cattlemen of the Panhandle, who had organized an association for the protection of their cattle interests known as the Canadian River Cattle Association, and of whom Mr. Charles Goodnight was one of the leading spirits, submitted a proposition to me to enter their employ, and, as their representative, to cooperate with the authorities of New Mexico with the view of suppressing and, putting an end to the wholesale raiding and stealing of cattle, which had been and was then carried on by Billy the Kid and his gang of desperadoes, of whom there were quite a number, and of whom a majority of the people in the localities were they were operating stood in fear and terror.

A never before published photograph of Pat Coghlan with what's believed to be his wife Anna and possibly his two nephews. *Courtesy of the Tularosa Village Historical Museum.*

> Billy the Kid found himself as one of the primary suppliers of acquired beef to the self-proclaimed "King of Tularosa:" Pat Coghlan. In May of 1880, a herd of sixty head of Panhandle beef was gathered at Portales before being driven south to the outskirts of White Oaks. This haul put $700 into the Kid's pocket. Despite the notoriety that Billy brought, Pat Coghlan profited the most from the stealing of Texas Panhandle cattle.
> Source: Utley, Robert. Billy the Kid: A Short and Violent Life. University of Nebraska Press, 1989. p. 133.

An agreement was arrived with the above-mentioned cattlemen under which I was given practically unlimited

The Death of Billy the Kid: Annotated Edition

authority to act for and represent them in all matters wherein their interests were affected in New Mexico, including authority to draw for all funds necessary for apprehending and prosecuting thieves and rustlers generally, and particularly those depredations of stock belonging to the Association, the only restriction being, of course, that I should proceed in a lawful manner.

Billy attempts to justify his livelihood in a letter addressed to Lew Wallace, dated December 12, 1880. During this time, Billy was under heavy pursuit by Garrett, and he undoubtedly sought to plead his case to the Governor. In the letter, Billy states, "I had been at Sumner Since I left Lincoln Making my living Gambling…There is no Doubt by what there is a great deal of Stealing going on in the Territory and a great deal of the Property is taken across the Plains as it is a good outlet but so far as my being at the head of a Band there is nothing of it in Several Instances I have recovered Stolen Property where there was no chance to get an Officer to do it."

Pursuant to this agreement, sometime in March 1881, I went to White Oaks, Lincoln County, New Mexico, which place was at that time quite a booming mining town, and was a sort of rendezvous for tough characters generally, including the following of the Kid, their friends and sympathizers, of whom there were many. It was here that I first met Pat Garrett, who was at that time sheriff of Lincoln County. After an interview with him, in which I explained the nature of my business in New Mexico, it was agreed that I should be commissioned as one of his deputies, which was done, and that we should co-operate in every way possible in an endeavor to suppress crime in that region generally, and particularly cattle rustling.

John W. Poe and Josh W. Slatten

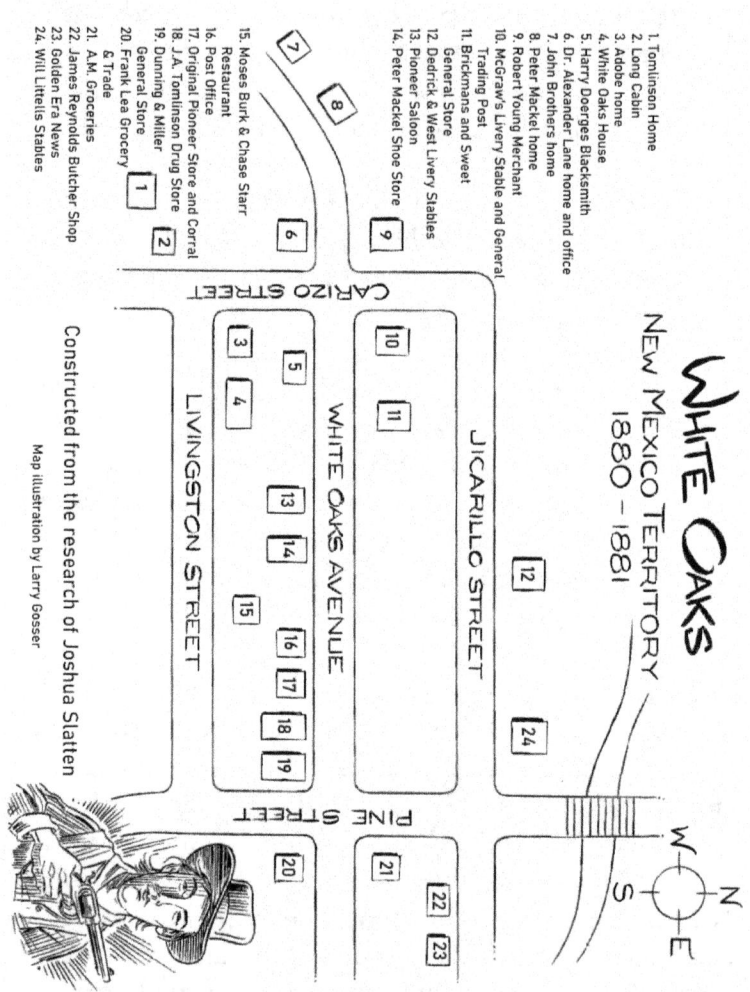

Map of White Oaks in 1881. This map was constructed through the independent research of this author to depict the layout of White Oaks during the time that Billy the Kid walked its streets. *Artwork by Larry Gosser.*

THE DEATH OF BILLY THE KID: ANNOTATED EDITION

The town of White Oaks as it appeared around the turn of the century. The viewer is looking south.

> At the time Poe resided in White Oaks, it was scarcely more than a mining camp. With the infusion of eastern influence and money, the mining town achieved incorporation in 1883 and prospered until it was eventually bypassed by the railroad in 1899. White Oaks held significance as a familiar haunt for Billy the Kid and his men and served as his operational base to unload stolen livestock acquired from the Texas Panhandle and other regions of New Mexico.
> Source:
> Haldane, Roberta. Gold-Mining Boomtown. University of Oklahoma Press, 2012. pp. 5-7.

It should be remembered that, at this particular time, the Kid was lying in jail, or rather held under guard, at Lincoln, the county seat, under sentence of death for murder, but had many sympathizers in the country and a number of followers still at large pursuing their trade of stealing cattle, committing robberies, and various other crimes, and that they were operating from the Panhandle of Texas through a great part of New Mexico and into Arizona.

John Poe, Pat Garrett and James Brent, ca. 1884. *Courtesy of The Historical Society for Southeast New Mexico.*

Poe and Garrett first crossed paths in April of 1880 in White Oaks. During Poe's stay in the town, he likely lodged at the White Oaks House Hotel. Serving as the town's inaugural hotel, the White Oaks House opened its doors on November 8th, 1880, under the direction of J.B. Collier, who aimed to establish the premier lodging facility in the burgeoning mining camp. The Las Vegas Morning Gazette reported that it "opened with a full house." Besides functioning as a hotel, the White Oaks House also offered rooms for permanent rental.

The Death of Billy the Kid: Annotated Edition

Source:
Poe, Sophie. Buckboard Days. *University of New Mexico Press, 1936. p.101.*
Author's independent research.

A cabinet card of Pat Garrett taken at Furlong & Crispell Studios, Las Vegas, New Mexico, September 10, 1881.

John W. Poe and Josh W. Slatten

At our first meeting it was agreed between Garrett and myself that I should make a trip to Tombstone, Arizona, which was then in its palmiest days as a mining camp, and where some of the stolen cattle from the Panhandle had been driven, which I hoped to recover, and that upon my return to White Oaks within a short time, we should meet again and confer together over the situation and decide upon what further course we were to pursue.

> *Milnor Rudulph informs Poe of his suspicion that Billy could have traveled to Tombstone, Arizona, potentially meeting his acquaintance, the notorious outlaw Johnny Ringo. Although there is no evidence to substantiate this claim, there are documented instances suggesting exchanges of stolen livestock between Lincoln County and Cochise County.*

This program was carried out, and on the day of our second meeting in White Oaks, sometime during the month of April, information came from Lincoln, some forty miles distant, that Billy the Kid had escaped from his guards, killing two of them, and was again at large. This occurred only a few days before the time set for the Kid's execution, and naturally caused a great deal of excitement throughout that region, as well as some rejoicing on the part of his friends and sympathizers.

> *Garrett neglects to mention any encounter with Poe in White Oaks during this period. He writes, "On the bloody 28th of April, I was at White Oaks. I left Lincoln on the day previous to meet engagements to receive taxes. Was at Las Tables on the 27th and went from there to White Oaks."*
>
> *Although Garrett does not explicitly state his purpose for visiting Las Tables, or "Board Town'" it is reasonable*

to infer that it was likely related to ordering timber for Billy's gallows. Las Tables, at that time, was a small ranching and lumbering community. Its Spanish name, meaning "the boards, planks," suggests its association with timber. The town site is situated approximately 20 miles directly. north of Lincoln, along Highway 246.

Source:

Garrett, Pat. The Authentic Life of Billy the Kid. *University of Oklahoma Press, 1959. p. 140.*

Julian, Robert. The Place Names of New Mexico. *University of New Mexico Press, 1996. p. 199*

The staircase that Billy ascended up, before making his famous escape, leaving Deputy Bell and Olinger's slain bodies in his wake. Photo taken 2024.

THE HUNT

Upon receipt of this information, Garrett immediately started for Lincoln, while it was agreed that I should remain on the lookout for the Kid at White Oaks for a time, as it was not known what direction he would take or where he would go after getting out of Lincoln.

> In *"The Authentic Life,"* Garrett offers additional insight into his return to Lincoln. He mentions that he first became aware of the Kid's escape on April 29th when he received a letter from the Fort Stanton postmaster, John C. Delaney. On the same day, he was also informed of the escape by Billy Nickey, who rode from Lincoln to deliver the news. Garrett then returned to Lincoln on April 30th, nearly 72 hours after Billy killed Bell and Olinger.
> Source: Authentic Life, p. 169.

Upon arriving at Lincoln on the night following the day of the escape, Garrett found that two of his deputies (Bob Olinger and a man named Bell) had been killed by the Kid, who, partly by means of a cunning ruse and partly by reason of the carelessness of the deputies, had broken into a room containing firearms, adjacent to where he was guarded, secured a six-shooter, by means of which he immediately proceeded to add two more to his already long list of victims.

JOHN W. POE AND JOSH W. SLATTEN

This image highlights what the courthouse looked like at the time that Billy the Kid made his famous escape. The staircase was not present at that time. The window that Billy shot Bob Olinger out of can be seen directly under the tree branch and above the door frame. Photo taken in the late 1920's. *Courtesy of the Historical Society for Southeast New Mexico.*

There are three theories regarding how Billy the Kid escaped from the courthouse that day. The commonly accepted version, told by Poe in this publication, aligns with Garrett's account in Authentic Life. Garrett describes the Kid as quickly and effortlessly rushing up the stairs ahead of the lagging Bell, forcing his way into the armory to grab a pistol and shoot Bell, who was "some twelve steps beneath." The second theory was first published in the 1926 book The Saga of Billy the Kid by Walter Noble Burns. Burns claims that the Kid snatched Bell's pistol while the two played Monte. With little to no evidence supporting it, this theory has been widely discredited as pure fiction on Burns' part. The third and most plausible explanation was originally advanced by Maurice Fulton, who argues that a friend of the Kid hid a pistol in the outhouse to aid his escape. After retrieving the pistol and reaching the top of the stairs, the Kid allegedly ordered Bell to surrender. When Bell refused and attempted to flee, he "turned and ran," leaving the Kid no choice but to shoot the escaping deputy.

In Sophie Poe's Buckboard Days, she writes, "There was one feature of the new home which I did not enjoy. The back stairway, up and down which I had to travel many times during the day, was still stained with blood, a grim reminder of the day two years before, when Billy the Kid had shot and killed his guard, James W. Bell.

Bell had been climbing those stairs and his body had fallen to the bottom of them." If Sophie Poe is correct, it would stand to reason that Garrett was in error when he claimed that Bell was shot at the landing of the staircase, "some twelve steps beneath," as the Kid fired. With blood found "up and down" the staircase, it is clear that Bell was not shot solely at the base of the stairs as Garrett described.

Sources:
Authentic Life, p.165.
Burns, Walter Noble. Saga of Billy the Kid. Doubleday Page & Camp; Company, 1926. p. 242
Buckboard Days. University of New Mexico Press, 1936. p. 205
Fulton, Maurice. History of the Lincoln County War. University of Arizona Press, 1997. p. 393

He then had compelled another man on the premises to secure a horse for him, upon which he rode away, leaving the people of the little town completely terrorized.

What remains of the small rock home of Jesus Padilla, where Billy sought a brief refuge following his escape. Photo taken in August, 2023.

When Billy rode out of Lincoln, several documented accounts describe the route he took and what he did along the way. While these accounts differ in detail, one consistent element emerges: a compilation of the sources suggests that Billy made a brief stop at the home of Jesus Padilla, located on the south side of the Capitan Mountains. Remnants of the small rock home can still be found today. After leaving the Padilla home, Billy supposedly crossed the Capitan Mountains and visited the home of Yginio Salazar's family in Las Tablas. At this point, John Meadows claims that Billy also stopped to see him at his ranch, located on the Penascos, approximately four miles below the current town of Elk. However, given Elk's location relative to Las Tablas and Fort Sumner, Meadows' claim appears highly improbable when viewed in conjunction with the other accounts.

Yginio Salazar in later years.

John W. Poe and Josh W. Slatten

Sources:
Anaya, Paco. I Buried Billy. *Early West Publications, 1991, p. 57.*

Taylor. "Facts Regarding the Escape of Billy the Kid," Frontier Times, *July 1936, p. 510.*

Wilson, John. Pat Garrett and Billy the Kid as I Knew Them. *University of New Mexico Press, 2004, p. 50.*

John Meadows later in life as he stands in the wagon yard of what was once Coghlan's Hotel in Tularosa, New Mexico. *Image courtesy of Joe Ben Saunders.*

Garrett at once organized several posses and scoured the country in all directions for several days in an endeavor to recapture his man, but failing to find any trace of him, finally gave up the hunt in the full belief that the Kid had gone to Old Mexico. According to my recollection this killing and escape occurred in the latter part of April, after which we were unable to learn anything whatever indicating the whereabouts of the Kid until the July following, notwithstanding the fact that we were constantly on the alert and made the most strenuous efforts to locate him.

THE DEATH OF BILLY THE KID: ANNOTATED EDITION

There has been considerable speculation regarding Pat Garrett's rationale for not immediately pursuing Billy the Kid after his escape and the killing of his guard in Lincoln. Many historians attribute Garrett's dismissive and seemingly nonchalant attitude towards chasing the Kid as a strategic move to bide his time, hoping to gather intelligence on the Kid's whereabouts. However, author and Pat Garrett historian David Thomas offers a compelling explanation for Garrett's delayed response.

It's often overlooked that Garrett and his wife had a two-month-old child at home during this time. Adelaida "Ida" Garrett was born on February 20, 1881, and was named after one of Garrett's sisters. This aspect sheds light on why Garrett might have been inclined to remain close to home, awaiting concrete evidence of the Kid's location before embarking on a pursuit.

Source: Trial, *p. 172.*

During the interval between the time of the Kid's escape and the time he was killed in July following, I continued to make headquarters at White Oaks, during which time I scoured the country thoroughly, finding many stolen cattle, also hides of stolen cattle which had been slaughtered, belonging to the Association I was representing; had a number of arrests made, prosecutions instituted, etc., being assisted in all this by Sheriff Garrett, who co-operated with me in every way possible, and whom I found to be a very brave and efficient officer.

Poe offers a highly complementary account of Garrett. However, in an April 19, 1947, interview with Sophie Poe, Garrett's sentiments towards Poe appear vastly different. Sophie Poe stated, "He (Garrett) became very bitter towards Poe in his later years, and one of Poe's

John W. Poe and Josh W. Slatten

Masonic brothers warned Poe that Garrett had threatened to kill him."

Source: *Robert N. Mullin files, Hailey Library, Midland Texas.*

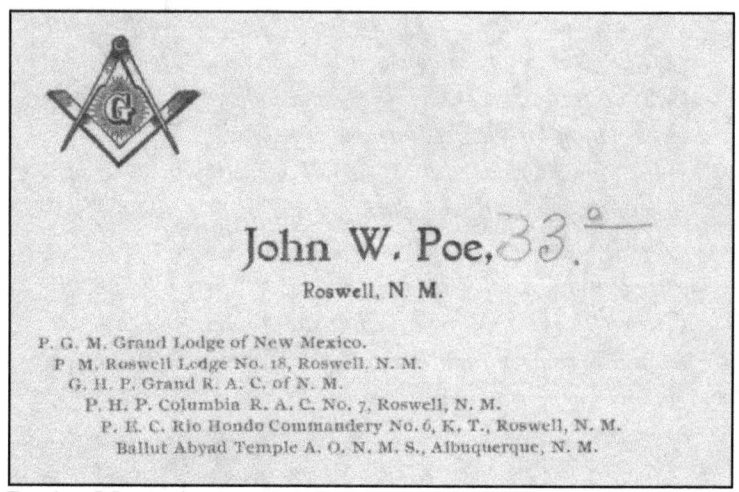

Poe's Masonic card. *Courtesy Historical Society for Southeast New Mexico.*

Sometime in the early part of July following the happenings above related, I was approached by a man in White Oaks, whom I had formerly known in Texas, who, although addicted to habits of dissipation, was a man of good principles, and who had, on previous occasions, shown a desire to assist me in the work I had in hand. This man told me a story in strict confidence. — as he probably felt that his life depended on its being treated in that respect — the gist of which was that, for want of a better place, he had for some time been occupying as sleeping quarters a vacant room in a certain livery stable, owned and operated by two men who were known to be friends of Billy the Kid; and that a short time previous, while in his sleeping quarters at night, he

The Death of Billy the Kid: Annotated Edition

had overheard a conversation between the two men, which convinced him that the Kid was yet in the country, making his headquarters at Fort Sumner, about a hundred miles distant from White Oaks.

> *The livery stable in question is the Dedrick and West Stable, which gained notoriety for its involvement in a counterfeit money scheme. Sam Dedrick partnered with William H. West to purchase the stables using counterfeit bills obtained from Billy Wilson. Wilson's circulation of 4, $100 counterfeit bills, attracted the attention of the United States Treasury Department. Despite initially prospering and being described by the* Las Vegas Morning Gazette *in 1880 as "well stocked" and conducting "big business," the stables' operation was short-lived due to increasing pressure from federal authorities. Consequently, there is no mention of it in the 1882 White Oaks business directory. Under mounting pressure, the Dedricks seemingly relocated to Socorro County briefly before moving elsewhere in the country.*
>
> *Source: The location of the stable is based on independent research conducted by this author.*

At two different times since his escape from Lincoln, the Kid had been in the vicinity of White Oaks and had met or communicated with the two men whose conversation he had overheard.

> *After escaping from the courthouse, it is conceivable, though not certain, that the Kid may have been in or near White Oaks. However, the only two accounts of his escape route come from Paco Anaya and John Meadows. While these accounts differ significantly, neither mentions Billy in the vicinity of White Oaks. Given the likelihood that Poe fabricated the account to protect Maxwell, it is reasonable*

to assume that he also fabricated the claim of Billy being in the vicinity of White Oaks.

Billy the Kid on his way to hang in Lincoln. *Illustration by Larry Gosser.*

I was somewhat skeptical as to the correctness of this information, as it seemed almost unbelievable that the Kid, after nearly three months had elapsed from the time of his escape with a price on his head, and under sentence of death, would still be lingering in the country. However, in view of the peculiar conditions then existing in the country, and the fact that the Kid had many friends and sympathizers who looked upon him as a hero and who would probably shelter and protect him, I came to the conclusion that there was possibly truth in the story which had been told me.

> *Billy didn't share Poe's confidence in his popularity in the area. When he was escorted to Lincoln from Mesilla, he had a brief moment to speak to the Newman's Semi-Weekly. "He was sure his guards would not hurt him unless a rescue should be attempted, and he was certain that would not be done unless, perhaps, 'those fellows over at*

White Oaks came out to take me,' meaning to kill him. It was, he said, about a stand-off whether he was hanged or killed in the wagon."

Source: Newman's Semi-Weekly *(Las Cruces, New Mexico), April 10, 1881.*

The Wagon Ruts can still be seen on the road between Las Cruces and Tularosa. It was along this road that Billy was transported to be hanged following his trial in Mesilla. Photo taken 2022.

I immediately went to the county seat [Lincoln], where I laid the matter before the sheriff as it had been told me.

This marks the first instance where Poe and Garrett's accounts diverge. While Poe takes credit for the information that led them towards Fort Sumner, Garrett attributes it to letters from Wayne Brazil, indicating Billy's presence in and around Fort Sumner.

Both Garrett and Poe claim to have obtained their information from independent sources. However, the truth may be more clandestine. In an interview between renowned Garrett historian Leon Metz and Cliff McKinney, son of "Kip" McKinney, Cliff revealed that Pete Maxwell dispatched a "trusted vaquero" to White Oaks to inform both Poe and Garrett of the Kid's whereabouts near Fort Sumner. Fearing reprisal, Maxwell orchestrated the story that Poe received the tip from an anonymous source in White Oaks.

Peter "Pedro" Maxwell, otherwise known as "Don Chootme" and Henry Leis.

Sophie Poe expands on this narrative, recounting a late-night visit from a friend of Poe's, known as "Quinn," who disclosed, "I know where the Kid is! I've been sleeping here and there, wherever I could. A few nights ago, I turned in on the hay in a livery stable. The two partners running the

place are friends of the Kid. Well, I was waked by them talking, and when I heard his name mentioned I listened close. Mr. Poe - the Kid's not in Mexico! He never has been in Mexico. He's over at Fort Sumner hiding in his querida's house. And he's been right here in White Oaks since he broke out. That's what those fellows said."

A young Paulita Maxwell. Unknown date.

Pete Maxwell likely harbored unease over the attention his younger sister Paulita received from a wanted murderer. Both Billy and Paulita were infatuated with each other, a sentiment conveyed through correspondence between Sheriff James Southwick of Mesilla and Pat Garrett. While the Kid was incarcerated in Mesilla, he exchanged letters with "his girl, Miss Maxwell." Southwick cautioned Garrett to keep a vigilant eye on Paulita, noting that "she was clearly stuck on Billy."

Source:
Buckboard Days, *p. 104.*
Dworkin, Mark. American Myth Maker. *University of Oklahoma Press, 2015. p. 31.*

The sheriff was much more skeptical as to the truth of the story than I was — said he could not believe there was any truth in what the White Oaks man had told me. He finally said that, if I desired it, he would go to Roswell, where we would find one of his deputies named McKinney, and from there the three of us would go to Fort Sumner with the determination of unearthing the Kid if he were there.

Thomas Christopher "Kip" McKinney and his wife, Teresa Smith McKinney in later years. *Special thanks to the family of Kip McKinney who shared the photo.*

The Death of Billy the Kid: Annotated Edition

J.S. Lea, unknown Date. *Courtesy of the Historical Society for Southeast New Mexico*

Another contradiction between Garrett and Poe's accounts emerges regarding the location where they picked up Garrett's second Deputy, Kip McKinny. Garrett writes that all three men departed from Lincoln, while Poe claims that he and Garrett rode into Roswell to pick up McKinney. A third perspective on the events comes from J. Smith Lea, who asserted to have served as a deputy under Garrett and recounted his version of the story to the San Angelo Evening Standard *on May 16.*

"One day we heard that Billy the Kid was at Fort Sumner," Mr. Lea stated. "The three deputies drew straws *as to who would accompany Garrett and John Poe, and Kip McKinney won. In order to avoid suspicion of their destination, Pat Garrett and his deputies left Lincoln at night, initially traveling in a different direction before looping around towards Roswell. From Roswell, they proceeded by night marches to the old government fort at Fort Sumner."*

Source: San Angelo Evening Standard, *May 16, 1930.*

This was agreed upon, and the following day we went to Roswell, where we found McKinney, who expressed his disbelief in the White Oaks story, but who willingly joined us for the expedition to Fort Sumner, which place is some eighty miles distant from Roswell.

Early day Roswell from a distance. *Courtesy Historical Society for Southeast New Mexico.*

Historians and skeptics of the conventional story surrounding the Kid's demise have often questioned why Garrett would embark on the pursuit with only two deputies, especially ones who had never encountered the Kid before. The answer is relatively straightforward. Just three months earlier, Billy had left two highly capable deputies dead in his wake. The number of individuals willing to pursue the Kid after such a violent act was likely limited. Finding qualified individuals who were not only willing to

THE DEATH OF BILLY THE KID: ANNOTATED EDITION

pursue the Kid but also familiar with his appearance would have been even more challenging. At the time, Pat Garrett had only a few deputies, none of whom had ever seen the Kid before.

The Lea-Bonney Company store is the structure located closest to the viewer. Unknown date. *Courtesy of the Historical Society for Southeast New Mexico.*

After a few hours spent in Roswell arranging for the trip, we started about sundown, riding out of town in a different direction from that we intended to travel later, as it was absolutely necessary to keep the public in ignorance of our plans if anything was to be accomplished.

> *A 1930 account of Deputy J. Smith Lea's life, published in The* Roswell Daily Record *on May 3, describes what happened when Garrett, Poe, and McKinney arrived in Roswell before heading north to Fort Sumner:*
>
> *"Pat Garrett, after he had located Billy the Kid at Ft. Sumner, left Lincoln at night with his deputies Kip McKinney and John W. Poe, coming to Roswell, where he purchased his ammunition from C.D. Bonney, who was*

operating a store at the time where the Chamber of Commerce now stands."

C.D. Bonney arrived in Roswell in June of 1881 at the age of twenty-one. He purchased an interest from Captain J. C. Lea in Roswell's pioneer store, which then became known as the Lea-Bonney Company.

Sources: Bonney, Cecil. Looking Over My Shoulder: Seventy Five Years in the Pecos Valley. *Hall-Poorbaugh Press, 1971, p. 1.*

After we were well out of the settlement, we changed our course and rode in the direction of Fort Sumner until about midnight, when we stopped, picketed our horses, and slept on our saddle-blankets for the remainder of the night. The next day we rode some fifty or fifty-five miles, halting late in the evening at a point in the sand hills some five or six miles out from Fort Sumner, where we again picketed our horses and slept until morning.

RECONNOITERING FORT SUMNER

It was agreed that as I was not known in Fort Sumner, while the other two men were, Garrett having a year or two previously resided there, I should ride into the place with the object of reconnoitering the ground and gathering such information as was possible that might aid us in our purpose, while the other two men were to remain out of sight in the sand hills for the day, and in case of my failure to return to them before night, they were to meet me after darkness came on at a certain point agreed on some four miles out of Fort Sumner.

In the September 10, 1879 issue of the Clyde (Kansas) Herald, *an article titled "A New Mexican Town" vividly describes what Poe must have seen upon riding into the small village:*

"Fort Sumner has lost much of its former glory but remains an attractive place. A broken flagstaff and a solitary cannon alone mark the parade ground. The commissary building has deteriorated into the residence of an elderly African American washerwoman, and the adjutant general's office is now utilized as a storeroom and post office by Messrs. Garrett & Smith - the former an old buffalo hunter, and the latter the greatest beaver hunter of

the Southwest. There is another store there kept by a Mexican, who, due to seldom stocking anything to sell, receives little patronage. The population of the place is probably 200 souls, with the majority being Mexican. They all reside in houses belonging to the Maxwell estate, and the only compensation they provide for their use is an occasional coat of whitewash."

Fort Sumner during its time as an active military post. The building on the left side of the image closest to the camera would eventually house Hargrove's Saloon.

In pursuance of this plan, I next morning left my companions and rode into town, where I arrived about ten o'clock. Fort Sumner at that time had a population of only some two or three hundred people, nearly all of whom were natives or Mexicans, there being not more than one or two dozen Americans in the place, a majority of whom were tough or undesirable characters, in sympathy with the Kid, while the remainder stood in terror of him.

The Death of Billy the Kid: Annotated Edition

Where Poe concludes that some of the population of Fort Sumner "stood in terror of him" is uncertain. There are no documented reports of anyone in Fort Sumner living in terror because of his presence in the village.

When I entered the town, I noticed that I was being watched from every side, and soon after I had stopped and hitched my horse in front of a store which had a saloon annex, a number of men gathered around and began to question me as to where I was from, where bound, etc. I answered with as plausible a yarn as I was able to give, telling them I was from White Oaks, where I had been engaged in mining, and was on my way to the Panhandle, where I had formerly lived.

This story seemed to allay their suspicions to some extent, and I was invited to join in a special drink at the saloon, which I did, being very careful that I absorbed but a very small portion of the liquor.

Two saloons were operational during that time: Bob Hargrove's and Beaver Smith's Saloon. Bob Hargrove's is notable as the location where the Kid killed Joe Grant in January of 1880. Situated on the northeast corner of the parade ground, it was initially used by the military as the quartermaster store. Bob Hargrove appears on the 1880 federal census at Fort Sumner under the name W. I. Hargrove, with a given age of 32.

The second saloon that Poe may have visited was Beaver Smith's. Located on the southwest corner of the parade ground, it gained fame as the site where the famous tintype of Billy the Kid was taken. "Old Beaver Smith," renowned as "the greatest beaver hunter of the southwest," departed Fort Sumner around late 1881 or early 1882, relocating to Austin, Texas. In Austin, he was arrested for the theft of a wagon, two horses, and $50 cash from a local woman.

John W. Poe and Josh W. Slatten

Serving a two-year sentence at the Rusk Penitentiary in Eastern Texas, he was released with time served on March 29, 1884, and subsequently disappeared from public record. However, in 1891, a man named George Fulton applied for a Civil War Pension in New Mexico, revealing that his real name was Albert H. Smith. Fulton passed away in 1899, with newspapers describing him as an old pioneer who arrived in New Mexico between 1846 and 1850 as a member of the Dragoons.

Source:

The Saline County Journal, *Saline, Kansas, September 4, 1879.*

U.S. Civil War Pension Index: General Index to Pension Files,
1861-1934.

Austin American Statesman, *Austin, Texas, April 6, 1882.*

Texas, U.S., Convict and Conduct Registers, 1875-1954.

This operation was repeated several times, as was the custom in those days, after which I went to a near-by restaurant for something to eat. After I had eaten a square meal, I loitered about the village for some three hours, chatting casually with people I met in the hope of learning something definite as to whether or not the Kid was there or had recently been there, but was unable to learn anything further than that the people with whom I conversed were still suspicious of me.

Poe claims that his identity in Fort Sumner as well as his intended purpose had gone unknown; however, there is reason to believe that Poe had tipped his hand and Billy was, in fact, aware of the presence of Garrett and his deputies. John Collins (possibly an alias of Abraham

The Death of Billy the Kid: Annotated Edition

Graham), a man who had allegedly been acquainted with Billy and ridden with him for a short time, encountered Billy on the 14th of July and warned him that he had seen Poe in the vicinity and suspected that Garrett was close by. Collins claims that Billy casually disregarded his warning.

Source: Kemp, Ben. Dead Men Who Rode Across the Border. *Rasch Collection.*

John Collins. *Ancestry*.

It was plain that many of them were on the alert, expecting something to happen. In fact, there was a very tense situation in Fort Sumner on that day, as the Kid was at that very time hiding in one of the houses there, and if the object of my visit had become known, I should have stood no chance for my life whatever.

> *Where Poe acquired this information from or if there is any truth to it is unknown. Garrett makes no mention of the Kid hiding out that day in Fort Sumner while Poe made his inquiries about the town. In Paco Anaya's account, detailed in* "I Buried Billy," *Paco talks of Billy spending the day leading up to his death at the Yerby Ranch, located 15 miles east of town. It's entirely possible that Poe added*

73

this detail to the story to try and build suspense and make it appear that he was in greater danger than he might have actually been in.

Source:
I Buried Billy, *p.124*.

The Yerby Ranch as it appears today. The site has been untouched by time since the days of the Kid. The site was located by the author in February of 2022. The corral posts can still be clearly seen. Photo taken 2022.

The Death of Billy the Kid: Annotated Edition

It was understood, when I left my companions in the morning, that in case of my being unable to learn any definite information in Fort Sumner, I was to go to the ranch of a Mr. Rudulph (an acquaintance and a supposed friend of Garrett's), which was located some seven miles north of Fort Sumner at a place called Sunnyside, with the purpose of securing from him, if possible, some information as to the whereabouts of the man we were after.

Sunnyside New Mexico. Unknown date.

The original town of Sunnyside once sat adjacent to what is now the town of Fort Sumner. Sunnyside operated as its own independent town with its own post office. In April of 1907, after Sunnyside was devastated by a storm, it was allowed to incorporate itself into the current town of Fort Sumner.

Source: The Fort Sumner Review. *Library of Congress*

Accordingly, I started from Fort Sumner about the middle of the afternoon for Rudulph's ranch, arriving there some time before night.

John W. Poe and Josh W. Slatten

John Poe's visit to the Rudulph Ranch is also described in similar detail in "LosBilitos": The Story of "Billy the Kid" And His Gang. *In this account, Rudulph doesn't mention Poe wishing to stay the night and makes no reference to being in "mortal terror" of Billy, as Poe describes. Instead, Rudulph tells Poe that he suspects Billy could have made his way over to Tombstone, Arizona, where he may have met up with his friend, the notorious outlaw Johnny Ringo.*

Source: Branch, Louis Leon. "Los Bilitos": The Story of 'Billy the Kid' And His Gang. *Carlton Press, 1980. pp. 246-248.*

Milnor Rudulph, taken around the time of the Kid's death. (Note that Poe spells his name Rudolph.)

I found Mr. Rudolph at home, presented the letter of introduction which Garrett had given me, and told him that I wished to stop overnight with him. After reading the letter, he said that Garrett was a very good friend of his, and that he would be very glad to furnish me with accommodations for the night, invited me into his house, took charge of my horse, etc.

The Death of Billy the Kid: Annotated Edition

Garrett took a gamble by assuming Poe would be safe when he sent him to visit Milnor Rudulph at his ranch. Milnor and his wife Maria had sheltered Billy numerous times over the past few years. Maria had taken a liking to the young outlaw and was quick to provide accommodations to him and his men when they would stop by the ranch. While always gracious, Billy was her favorite and would be permitted to stay and eat in the house while the others were only allowed to stay in the bunkhouse. However, this luxury would eventually run out for the Kid. Towards the end of his life, the Rudulphs had grown tired of Billy's outlaw ways. Upon Billy's last visit to the ranch, he was required, along with his men, to hand over their firearms if they were to stay the night. The hospitality that Billy once enjoyed was no longer there, and they were only allowed to sleep in the barn for the night. The following morning, a somber exchange occurred between Billy and Milnor Rudulph: "Los Bilitos woke up before sunrise, fed and watered their horses early, and afterwards saddled them and started out. Not smiling, a disquieting, self-denouncing look in his eyes, Billy looked straight at Milnor Rudulph as he left, saying: 'Mil gracias por todo, amigo-adios!' The next time Rudulph would see him, he would be lying on Don Pedro Maxwell's floor, a bullet hole through his chest."
Source: Los Bilitos, *pp.146, 182.*

After supper was over, I engaged in conversation with him, discussing the conditions in the country generally, and after some little time, I led up to the escape of Billy the Kid from Lincoln, and remarked that I had heard a report that the Kid was hiding in or about Fort Sumner. Upon my making this remark, the old gentleman showed plainly that he was getting nervous; said he had heard that such a report was about, but did not believe it, as the Kid was in his opinion too shrewd to be caught lingering in that part of the country with a price upon his head and knowing that the officers of the law were diligently seeking him.

By this time I was pretty well convinced that Mr. Rudolph was naturally well-intentioned, but like so many others, was in almost mortal terror of the Kid, and on account of this fear, was very reluctant to say anything whatever about him. I then told him plainly the object of our errand - that I had come to him with the express purpose of learning, if possible, where the Kid could be found; that we believed he was hiding in or near Fort Sumner, and that Garrett, the sheriff, expected that he (Rudolph) would be able to put us on the right trail. Upon my making this statement, Mr. Rudolph apparently became more nervous and excited than ever, and reiterated his reasons for believing that the Kid was not in that part of the country, and showed plainly — so it seemed to me — that he was not only embarrassed but alarmed. The truth was, we afterwards learned, that he was well aware of the fact that the Kid was then, and had been for some time, hiding about Fort Sumner, but his dread of the Kid caused him to make misleading statements while withholding facts.

Charles Rudulph recounts the visit between Poe and his father Milnor: "We haven't seen him for quite a while. I think it was late in the fall when he stopped by last, and we haven't seen him since...Billy."

There is nothing to indicate during Milnor's conversation with Poe, nor when in Fort Sumner the following day, that he was in fear of Billy or had any indication that he had been in the area.

Source: ibid.

Site of Rudulph Ranch today.

Darkness was now approaching, and I said to Mr. Rudolph that inasmuch as myself and my horse were by this time pretty well rested, having had a good feed, I had changed my mind, and, instead of stopping overnight with him, would saddle up and ride during the cool of the evening to meet my companions. This I accordingly did, much, I thought, to the relief of Rudolph. I rode directly to the point where I had agreed to meet my companions, and, strange to say, as I approached the point from one direction, they came into view from the other, so that we did not have to wait for each other. This proved to be a night of strange happenings with us, however, all the way through. We here held a consultation as to what further course we should pursue. I had spent the day in endeavoring to learn something definite of the whereabouts of the man we wanted, but without success, save that from the actions of the people I had met at Fort Sumner, together with Mr. Rudolph's nervous and excited manner, I was more firmly convinced than ever that our man was in the vicinity.

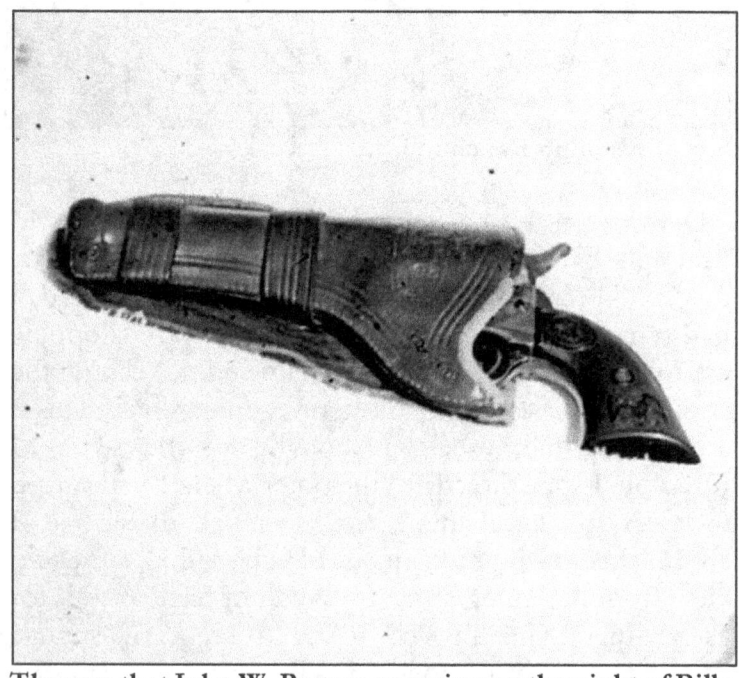

The gun that John W. Poe was wearing on the night of Billy the Kid's death. The pistol is now in the hands of a private collector. *Photo courtesy of the Mullin files.*

STRANGE SEQUECE OF HAPPENINGS THE NIGHT OF JULY 14, 1881

Garrett seemed to have but little confidence in our being able to accomplish the object of our trip, but said that he knew the location of a certain house occupied by a woman in Fort Sumner which the Kid had formerly frequented, and that if he was in or about Fort Sumner, he would most likely be found entering or leaving this house sometime during the night.

> *If this were true, Pete Maxwell could have been one of the few individuals who could have provided such information about the Kid's exact whereabouts. Perhaps this was the reason why Garrett went into Maxwell's bedroom that night, potentially to gather more intelligence or to confirm Maxwell's involvement, only to get lucky and stumble upon the Kid before he had a chance to organize a more elaborate ambush.*
>
> Source: Speculation based on the circumstances and historical context.

Garrett proposed that we go into a grove of trees near the town, conceal our horses, then station ourselves in the peach orchard at the rear of the house, and keep watch on who might come or go. This course was agreed upon, and we entered the peach orchard about nine o'clock that night, stationing ourselves in the gloom or shadow of the peach trees, as the moon was shining very brightly.

John Cloud Jacobs, ca. 1930.

While not mentioned by Poe, Pat Garrett interjects a detail into the story at this point that has been overlooked by historians. Garrett mentions that prior to entering the peach orchard, they came upon a man who had set up camp. To Poe's surprise, it was an old friend of his from Texas. Garrett identifies the man only as Jacobs. This man was, in fact, John Cloud Jacobs. The two men were close friends and business partners in Texas when they were buffalo skinners. Neither Poe nor Garrett make any more mention of Jacobs in their personal recollections of that night.

John Jacobs went on to lead an accomplished life after relocating to San Antonio. Before his passing in 1932, he became famous for raising and training polo ponies. The most famous of which was named "Jacobs" and was inducted into the Polo Hall of Fame in 2022.

Source:
Authentic Life, *p.144*

The Death of Billy the Kid: Annotated Edition

The Hearne Democrat, *"Tells of Buffalo Hunting in the Old West,"* February 2, 1935

We kept up a fruitless watch here until sometime after eleven o'clock, when Garrett stated that he believed we were on a cold trail; that he had very little faith in our being able to accomplish anything when we started on the trip. He proposed that we leave the town without letting anyone know that we had been there in search for the Kid.

The peach orchard factors into the events of that night more than one might first realize. Both Poe and Garrett make mention of the orchard, with Poe indicating that they were there for the purposes of conducting surveillance, while Garrett only mentions entering the orchard without stating a specific purpose. What is interesting is that Poe makes no mention of anything suspicious occurring during this time. However, Garrett refers to seeing what he would later learn was none other than the Kid. Garrett states, "We approached these houses cautiously, and when within earshot, heard the sound of voices conversing in Spanish. We concealed ourselves quickly and listened; but the distance was too great to hear words, or even distinguish voices. Soon a man arose from the ground, in full view, but too far away to recognize. Little as we suspected, this man was the Kid."

Here is where the story gets interesting. Jesus Silva, in an interview later in life, makes mention of the peach orchard and some startling details that, if true, change the entire dynamics of the Kid's death. Silva states, "When I got back, Billy and me sat there and drank and talked for several minutes. While we sat there, Pat Garrett and the other sheriffs were hiding behind the trees with their guns pointed at us. The other sheriffs wanted to kill Billy, but Pat wouldn't let them because I was there."

Is it possible that Billy and Silva were the voices that Garrett mentioned hearing? One has to ask, how did Silva know that Poe and McKinney wanted to shoot Billy at that time and that Garrett, in fact, wouldn't allow it? This information could have only been related to Silva after the shooting if it were true.

Source:

Authentic Life, pp. 144,145

The Amarillo Daily News, "I Was with Billy the Kid That Night Just Before Pat Garrett Killed 'im' Says Man Who Knew Fearless Gunman," Friday, November 13,1936.

Jesus Silva, ca. 1910. Silva was one of the key players in the aftermath of the death of Billy the Kid. He claimed to make the Kid's coffin and assisted in digging his grave. He died in Fort Sumner in 1940.

I then proposed that, before leaving, we should go to the residence of Peter Maxwell, a man who up to that time I had never seen, but who, by reason of his being a leading citizen and having large property interests, should, according to my reasoning, be glad to furnish such information as he might have to aid us in ridding the country of a man who was looked on as a scourge and curse by all law-abiding people.

The Maxwell home. The Kid was killed in the room located on the ground floor corner room closest to the camera. Date unknown. *Photo courtesy of the Mullin files.*

> *Poe again continues to indicate that Garrett is less than enthusiastic about their ability to apprehend the Kid or even that he is in the area. In* "Authentic Life," *Garrett leads the reader to believe that he instructed Poe and McKinney to approach the Maxwell residence with him. Garrett displayed an air of confidence as he claimed to instruct Poe and McKinney to remain vigilant as he addressed Pete Maxwell inside the residence that once served as the officers' quarters.*
> Source: Authentic Life, *145*

Garrett agreed to this, and thereupon led us from the orchard by circuitous by-paths to Maxwell's residence, which was a building formerly used as officers' quarters during the days when a garrison of troops had been maintained at the fort. Upon our arriving at the residence (a very long, one-story adobe, standing end to and flush with the street, having a porch on the south side, which was the direction from which we approached, the premises all being enclosed by a paling fence, one side of which ran parallel to and along the edge of the street up to and across the end of the porch to the corner of the building.

> *Poe's description of the Maxwell home is important. He indicates that it is a one-story structure, not the two-story image we are accustomed to seeing in the familiar image. If the structure was indeed single-story, then it would imply that the renovation had not yet been completed. Lucian Maxwell purchased the property from the U.S. Military for $5,000. His original offer of $750 was refused.*
> Source:
> The Santa Fe New Mexican, *May 21, 1870.*
> Trial, *p.9*

Garrett said to me, 'This is Maxwell's room in this corner. You fellows wait here while I go in and talk to him' Thereupon he stepped onto the porch and entered Maxwell's room through the open door (left open on account of the extremely warm weather), while McKinney and myself stopped on the outside. McKinney squatted on the outside of the fence, and I sat on the edge of the porch in the small open gateway leading from the street onto the porch.

The Death of Billy the Kid: Annotated Edition

The importance of the layout of Pete Maxwell's room at the time of the Kid's death cannot be overstated. While it may seem trivial at first, establishing whether or not there was an interior door would help solve a great deal of mystery behind that night. What we do know for certain is that the home was renovated, but to what extent and when is unknown. Many historians have contended that Billy may have been staying inside the home at the time he was killed, therefore concluding that he would have entered the bedroom from the interior door and not by backing into the exterior door that led directly into Pete's bedroom. Considering that we know that Billy and Paulita were sweet on one another, it's not beyond reason to come to such a conclusion. History is ever evolving and in recent years there has been quite a bit of momentum generated from a variety of Billy the Kid authors supporting the notion that Billy came from inside the residence and not from the home of Celsa Gutierrez like both Poe and Garrett contend.

There are two glaring problems with the idea that Billy came from within the residence. In the Las Vegas Gazette, *July 19, 1881* we have a diagram of Pete Maxwell's bedroom. Both Garrett and Pete Maxwell made their way to Las Vegas just after the Kid's death. It stands to reason that this diagram was given by one of them. The interesting thing we take away from this diagram is that there is no interior door shown. Enough detail was given to show where all the windows were located so it seems reasonable that an interior door would not have been omitted. The second problem comes in an almost identical drawing that was located in the Mullin files at the Hailey Library in Midland Texas. Robert Mullin had a sketch drawn up of Maxwell's bedroom and labeled it "as per Burns account." Interestingly enough, both diagrams match nearly perfectly, neither of which show an interior door. If these two independent accounts are to be believed, it's safe to *say that the original floor plan had been changed during the renovation, removing the interior door and adding the exterior door that led to the porch. This small, yet significant detail debunks the notion that Billy came from inside the home and reinforced the probability that Billy came upon Garrett and his party just as history has recorded, from outside.*

An additional source that helps lend credence to the notion that the home was still a single-story establishment at the time of the Kid's death comes from Charles Siringo. He states; "He (Pete Maxwell) lived in a long, one story adobe building, which had been the U.S. officers' quarters when the soldiers were stationed there." While Siringo's credibility has been questioned from time to time, there's no reason to embellish or be untruthful about the design of Maxwell's home at that time. Furthermore, Siringo's book was published in 1920, over a decade before Poe's account of that night and description of the home was widely published and accessible.

Source: History of Billy the Kid, *p.128*

It should be mentioned here that up to this moment I had never seen Billy the Kid, nor Maxwell, which fact, in view of the events transpiring immediately afterward, placed me at an extreme disadvantage.

It was probably not more than thirty seconds after Garrett had entered Maxwell's room, when my attention was attracted, from where I sat in the little gateway, to a man approaching me on the inside of and along the fence, some forty or fifty steps away. I observed that he was only partially dressed and was both bareheaded and barefooted, or rather, had only socks on his feet, and it seemed to me that he was fastening his trousers as he came toward me at a very brisk walk.

The Death of Billy the Kid: Annotated Edition

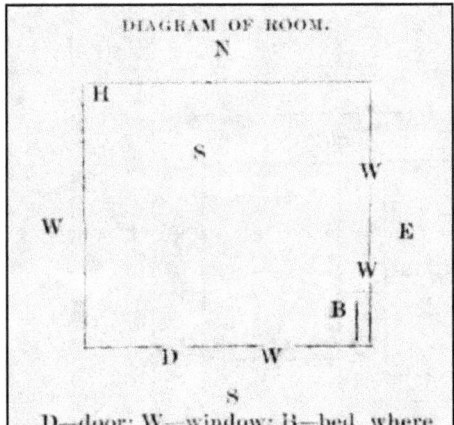

The layout of Maxwell's Bedroom the night of the Kid's death. Diagram from *The Las Vegas Gazette*, July 19, 1881. Illustration courtesy of the Mullin files.

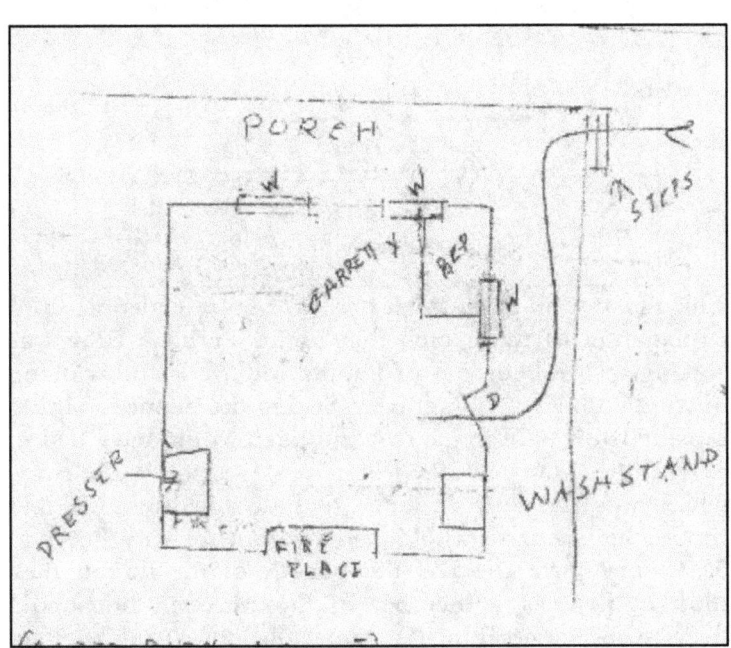

An additional layout of Maxwell's bedroom as it would look the night of the Kid's death, as described by Walter Noble Burns. Illustration courtesy of the Mullin files.

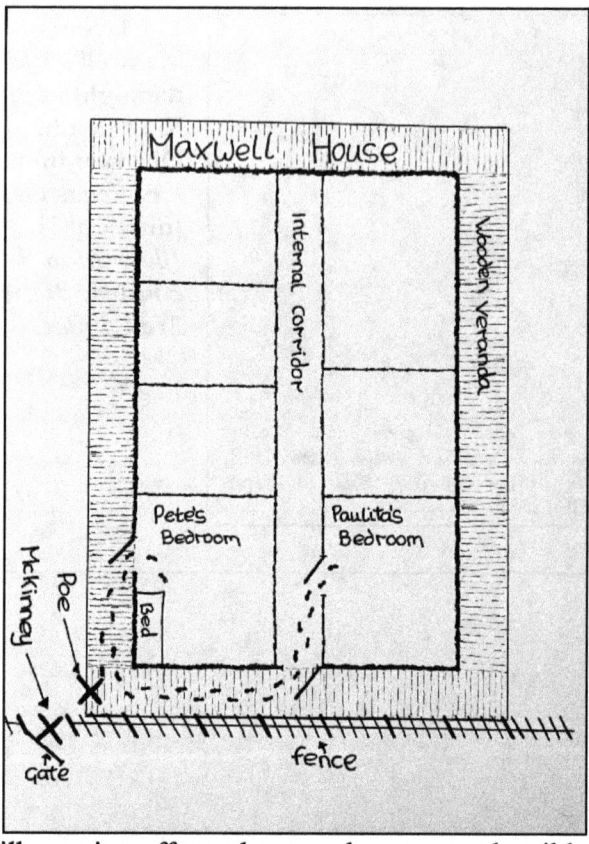

This illustration offers what may be a more plausible third explanation of the events that night. Perhaps Billy was staying in the bedroom of Paulita Maxwell, and walking outside on his way to get beef. Seeing the deputies sitting outside, Billy, still in his stocking feet, would have had to enter Pete Maxwell's bedroom via the porch doorway, which was the only entrance to Pete's bedroom at that time. This scenario would also account for why Poe and McKinney gave the Kid the benefit of the doubt: they thought he was a member of the Maxwell household because he came from the Maxwell house itself. A man walking out of the Maxwell home and asking deputies who they were would elicit a much different response than a man approaching them from the exterior and drawing a weapon.

The Death of Billy the Kid: Annotated Edition

The gun that killed Billy the Kid. Serial number 55093, 1880, 44-40 caliber 7 ½ inch barrel. The pistol was confiscated from Billy Wilson when he, Dave Rudabaugh, Tom Picket and Billy the Kid were captured at Stinking Springs. The pistol was used to kill Billy the Kid before it was loaned to Tom Powers for exhibition at his Coney Island Saloon. The pistol was eventually recovered by Garrett's widow, Apolinaria Garrett before changing hands multiple times. It now sits in the private collection of Bill Koch after he purchased it in 2021. It sold for 6.3 million dollars, making it the most expensive firearm in history.

As Maxwell's was the one place in Fort Sumner that I had considered above suspicion of harboring the Kid, I was entirely off my guard, the thought coming into my mind that the man approaching was either Maxwell or some guest of his who might have been staying there. He came on until he was almost within arm's-length of where I sat, before he saw me, as I was partially concealed from his view by the post of the gate.

> *Poe's recollection of the Kid is surprisingly specific, given that he was observing from nearly twenty-five yards away in darkness. It seems implausible that the Kid could be walking briskly, fastening his trousers, and simultaneously holding a knife in one hand and a pistol in the other.*
>
> *Regarding the Kid's attire, most historical accounts indicate that he was barefoot at the time of his death. Paco*

*Anaya's account, however, presents a notable exception. He states, "When we dressed Billy, he had on his shoes, his pants and his shirt. Just his hat he did not have, or his vest" (*I Buried Billy, *p. 134). This discrepancy adds yet another layer of complexity to an already intricate narrative.*

Considering these inconsistencies, it is crucial for historians and researchers to critically evaluate each source, considering factors such as the reliability of the witness, the consistency of their recollections, and potential biases. The truth behind the Kid's exact actions and appearance may remain elusive, obscured by the passage of time and the variability of firsthand accounts.

Source: I Buried Billy, p.134

Upon his seeing me, he covered me with his six-shooter as quick as lightning, sprang onto the porch, calling out in Spanish, 'Quien es?' (Who is it?) — at the same time backing away from me toward the door through which Garrett only a few seconds before had passed, repeating his query, 'Who is it?' in Spanish several times.

Donald Cline's claim that Billy was unarmed at the time of his death contradicts most historical accounts, which assert that Billy was armed. He states that his pistol, a ".38 Colt double action Lightning, was found in Celsa Gutierrez's room." Cline continues to say that Poe made the statement that he had not seen the pistol until Garrett returned with it from Celsa Gutierrez' room. Without supporting evidence or citation, Cline's assertion lacks credibility.

Regarding the fate of Billy's pistol, Charles Siringo provides a different account, stating that the pistol was auctioned off the following spring in Lincoln. Siringo describes it as a "rubber-handled, double-action Colt's 41

The Death of Billy the Kid: Annotated Edition

caliber pistol" that Billy held in his hand when he was killed. The winning bid went to the county clerk, Billy Burt, for $13.50. This account aligns with other historical records and provides insight into the disposition of Billy's firearm after his death.

In evaluating historical accounts, it's essential to consider the reliability of the sources and the consistency of the information provided. Without corroborating evidence, claims such as Cline's should be approached with skepticism, while accounts supported by multiple sources, such as Siringo's, carry more weight.

Source:
Cline, Donald. Alias Billy the Kid. *Donald Cline. Sunstone Press, 1986, pp. 116, 118*
History of Billy the Kid, *p. 134*

At this I stood up and advanced toward him, telling him not to be alarmed, that he should not be hurt; and still without the least suspicion that this was the very man we were looking for. As I moved toward him trying to reassure him, he backed up into the doorway of Maxwell's room, where he halted for a moment, his body concealed by the thick adobe wall at the side of the doorway, from whence he put out his head and asked in Spanish for the fourth or fifth time who I was. I was within a few feet of him when he disappeared into the room.

The skepticism regarding why experienced lawmen like John Poe and McKinney allowed Billy the Kid to approach and gain the upper hand is understandable. However, it is crucial to contextualize the incident within the limitations and norms of 1881. Police tactics and training were rudimentary at best, and the lawmen were likely operating under different assumptions and situational awareness compared to modern standards.

John Poe's initial reaction, as he recounted, suggests that he did not immediately recognize the stranger as Billy the Kid. This is supported by his attempts to reassure the unknown person, indicating that Poe was cautious and possibly confused, rather than negligent. The entire event likely unfolded very quickly, leaving little time for detailed assessment or reaction. Poe's primary concern seemed to be avoiding unnecessary confrontation until the stranger's identity and intentions were clearer.

The Final - The Kid killed by the sheriff at Fort Sumner. This was one of the original images that appeared in Garrett's, *Authentic Life.*

After this, and until after the shooting, I was unable to see what took place on account of the darkness of the room, but plainly heard what was said on the inside. An instant after the man left the door, I heard a voice inquire in a sharp tone, 'Pete, who are those fellows on the outside?' An instant later a shot was fired in the room, followed immediately by what everyone within hearing distance thought were two other shots. However, there were only two shots fired, the third report, as we learned afterward, being caused by the rebound of the second bullet, which had struck the adobe wall and rebounded against the headboard of a wooden bedstead.

The headboard of Pete Maxwell's bed, next to which Pat Garrett sat beside on July 14, 1881.

There are several considerations to keep in mind when examining the accounts provided by Poe and Garrett. Initially, both men stated that three shots had been fired, but they later altered their stance, claiming that the third "shot" was actually nothing more than a ricochet. This shift in perspective was influenced by their inability to locate evidence of a third bullet.

Adding to the complexity is the examination of the Kid's pistol, which revealed a spent shell casing in the sixth chamber. Garrett explained this as a common safety practice of placing the hammer on an empty cartridge to prevent accidental discharge. While it was indeed common to keep the hammer on an empty chamber, utilizing a spent shell was not the customary practice. This suggests that Billy may have managed to fire off a shot, as a used casing implies an actual discharge rather than an empty precautionary measure.

Furthermore, it is important to recognize the distinct difference in sound between a gunshot and a ricochet. If all parties were well-versed in firearms—a reasonable assumption given their roles—they would likely have distinguished between the sound of a direct shot and that of a bullet striking another object.

Source: Authentic Life, *p.148.*

I heard a groan and one or two gasps from where I stood in the doorway, as of someone dying in the room. An instant later, Garrett came out, brushing against me as he passed. He stood by me close to the wall at the side of the door and said to me, 'That was the Kid that came in there onto me, and I think I have got him.' I said, 'Pat, the Kid would not come to this place; you have shot the wrong man.'

Upon my saying this, Garrett seemed to be in doubt himself as to whom he had shot, but quickly spoke up and said, 'I am sure that was him, for I know his voice too well to be mistaken.' This remark of Garrett's relieved me of considerable apprehension, as I had felt almost certain that someone whom we did not want had been killed.

Billy the Kid's death warrant.

John W. Poe and Josh W. Slatten

To understand John Poe's statement about Garrett shooting the wrong man, it's essential to consider the context in which it was made. Close examination of Poe's account reveals that he harbored significant doubts about the mission's success. Poe's narrative in "Authentic Life" reflects a deep skepticism about their chances of finding Billy the Kid in Fort Sumner that night.

Poe's own words illustrate his lack of confidence in the mission. He describes how even Garrett questioned whether they would find Billy in Fort Sumner. This doubt extended to the moment they encountered Billy, which explains Poe's initial hesitation when Garrett informed him about the Kid's death. Garrett had to reassure Poe by asserting, "I am sure that was him (Billy), for I know his voice too well to be mistaken." Poe admits that this remark from Garrett alleviated his considerable apprehension.

Further into his account, Poe corrects his earlier assumption about Maxwell's home being beyond suspicion. He acknowledges, "By this time, I had begun to realize that we were in a place that was not beyond suspicion, contrary to my initial belief about Maxwell's residence." This admission highlights Poe's evolving understanding of the situation as events unfolded.

Source: Authentic Life, p.148

A moment after Garrett came out of the door, Pete Maxwell rushed squarely onto me in a frantic effort to get out of the room, and I certainly would have shot him but for Garrett's striking my gundown, saying, 'Don't shoot Maxwell.'

'It was said that Don Pedro Maxwell, scared completely out of his wits, streaked past Pat Garrett over Billy's dead body and out the door. Trailing a cortege of blankets and bed clothes behind him, screaming in bloody terror, 'Don't

The Death of Billy the Kid: Annotated Edition

shoot me, don't shoot me!' Thereafter among his jesting friends, he was to be known instead of as Don Pedro, by the nickname of 'Don Chootme.'"
Source: Los Bilitos, *p.226*

As by this time I had begun to realize that we were in a place which was not above suspicion, such as I had thought the residence of Maxwell to be, and as Garrett was so positive that the Kid was inside, I came to the conclusion that we were up against a case of 'kill or be killed,' such as we had from the beginning realized would be the case whenever we came upon the Kid.

Poe and Garrett both emphasized the importance of maintaining control over the situation to avoid unnecessary risks when pursuing Billy the Kid. Their cautious approach is evident in Garrett's own words: "I, at no time, contemplated taking any chances which I could avoid by caution or cunning. The only circumstances under which we could have met on equal terms, would have been accidental, and to which I would have been an unwilling party".
They understood that meeting Billy on "equal terms" in an accidental encounter would likely result in a violent confrontation, which they wanted to avoid. Instead, they preferred to use "caution or cunning" to set the terms of any engagement, ensuring they had the upper hand. Garrett's recounting of the events reveals a lawman who was methodical and deliberate, valuing prudence over bravado.
Source: Authentic Life, *p. 113.*

I have ever since felt grateful that I did not shoot Maxwell, for, as I learned afterward, he was at heart a well-meaning, inoffensive man, but very timid. We afterward discovered that the Kid had frequently been at his house after his escape from Lincoln, but Maxwell stood in such terror of him that he did not dare to inform against him.

Deluvina Maxwell, a former Navajo slave and Maxwell servant. She was one of Billy's most devoted supporters. She died in Albuquerque in 1927. Her grave has been lost to time.

Deluvina Maxwell provides a different perspective from Poe's account regarding Billy the Kid's presence at Pete Maxwell's house. She asserts:

"Billy did not go to Maxwell's house often. He did not live there."

If Deluvina Maxwell's statement is accurate, it challenges the notion that Billy was staying at the Maxwell residence with Paulita on the night of his death. Instead, it supports the idea that Billy was coming from the Gutierrez residence, as Poe and Garrett contended.

The Death of Billy the Kid: Annotated Edition

This perspective from Deluvina Maxwell adds another layer to the mystery surrounding Billy the Kid's final moments and raises questions about the accuracy of various historical accounts.
Source:
Deluvina Maxwell, interview with J. Evetts Haley, June 24, 1927. Haley Library.

Pete Maxwell rarely spoke about the events of that night, but one account told by Col. Jack Potter provides insight into his experience. According to Potter, Maxwell shared his harrowing ordeal:
"I was riding along with Pete Maxwell and I asked him how he felt when he realized that he was trapped in bed between Sheriff Garrett and Billy the Kid. He drew up his reins, thought for a minute and said: 'I wish you had not asked me that question as I have tried to forget it all. I realized that I had three chances at being killed on the spot in the next instant. First by being between the two men; next, when the Kid fell forward, the butcher knife he had used to cut meat plunged close to my chest; and last, as I got out of bed to escape, I was stopped at the door by Deputy John Poe with his .45 in my stomach. The Deputy thought I was the Kid. I had a lot of explaining to do, pronto!'"
This account vividly illustrates the intense danger and confusion Maxwell faced during the encounter. Maxwell's fear of being caught in the crossfire, nearly being stabbed by Billy the Kid's butcher knife, and being mistaken for the Kid by Deputy Poe highlights the chaotic nature of that night. It also emphasizes the precarious position Maxwell found himself in, underscoring the life-or-death stakes of the confrontation.
Source: Burroughs, Jean. On the Trail. Museum of New Mexico Press, 1980, p. 139.

Jack Potter. Unknown Date. *Find a Grave*.

By this time all was quiet in the room, and as the darkness was such that we were unable to see what the conditions were on the inside or what the result of the shooting had been, we - after some rather forceful persuasion, indeed - induced Maxwell to procure a light, which he finally did by bringing an old-fashioned tallow candle from his mother's room at the far end of the building, passing by the rear to the end where the shooting occurred, and placing the candle on the window-sill from the outside.

> The differing accounts of the events following Billy the Kid's death highlight the complexity and uncertainty surrounding that night. Poe's and Garrett's versions differ significantly, and Paco Anaya's account adds another layer of complexity.
> Poe provides an unusual amount of detail about the lamp's origins, describing the process of entering the room and confirming Billy's death. Garrett, on the other hand, mentions entering the room but does not provide details on

how the decision to enter was made or who entered first, focusing more on the aftermath and confirmation of Billy's identity and death.

Paco Anaya claims that there was hesitation among the men to enter the room. He states that Deluvina Maxwell, the Indian cook, took the initiative by entering the room with a lighted lamp and placing it on a bureau near Billy's head.

The variations in these accounts can be attributed to the chaotic and tense nature of the moment, personal perspectives, and possible embellishments over time. Anaya's version adds a dramatic element by highlighting Deluvina Maxwell's courageous act, contrasting with the more procedural approach described by Poe and Garrett.

To further complicate matters, Deluvina Maxwell, in a letter written to J. Evetts Haley, contradicts Paco when she says, "I did not see Billy the night after he was killed, but saw him the following morning." Several other contemporary sources do place Deluvina at the scene that night. Considering she lived in the Maxwell home and was their servant, there is no reason to believe that she would not have been there that night. When reading the transcribed letter that Deluvina wrote to Haley, it needs to be considered that there could have been something lost in translation. The original handwritten copy has not surfaced, so we are relying on the transcribed version. Considering the fact that Deluvina's penmanship and English were more than likely poor, something very easily could have been lost in the translation of the original letter.

Deluvina's contradictions would not stop, as she was quoted in an interview given to Miguel Antonio Otero, at the same approximate time as the Haley letter: "He was afraid to go back to the room to make sure of whom he had shot! I went in and was the first to discover that he had killed my little boy."

Billy's Butcher Knife. The butcher knife the Kid was carrying when he was killed. It is a standard Green River skinning knife that measures 9 ¾ "overall. This photograph was given to this author by Frederick Nolan.

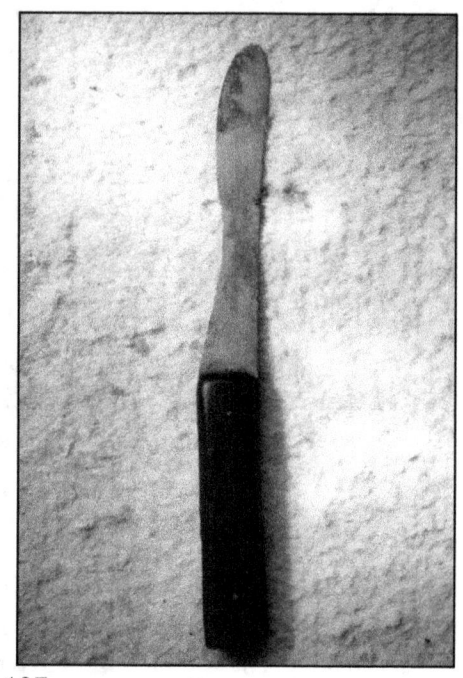

Source:
I Buried Billy, *p.127;*
Deluvina Maxwell, interview with J. Evetts Haley, June 24, 1927, Haley Library.
Otero, Miguel. *The Real Billy the Kid*. Arte Publico Press, 1998, p.116.

This enabled us to get a view of the inside, where we saw a man lying stretched upon his back dead, in the middle of the room, with a six-shooter lying at his right hand and a butcher-knife at his left. Upon examining the body, we found it to be that of Billy the Kid. Garrett's first shot had penetrated his breast just above the heart, thus ending the career of a desperado who, while only about twenty-three years of age at the time of his death, had killed a greater number of men than any of the many desperadoes and 'killers' I have known or heard of during the forty-five years I have been in the Southwest.

THE DEATH OF BILLY THE KID: ANNOTATED EDITION

Paco Anaya.

The knife that Billy was carrying the night he was killed remained unknown to historians until a privately printed book about the Jaramillo family of New Mexico was provided to historian Frederick Nolan. The narrative discusses the knife and how it came into the possession of the Swanson family. Mrs. Ollie Swanson was the daughter of Adelina Jaramillo Willborn, who was the daughter of Paulita Maxwell Jaramillo. Along with the knife were several affidavits authenticating its authenticity. One was written by Deluvina Maxwell in 1926, and the other by Celsa Gutierrez's son, Candido. In Candido's affidavit, he affirms that he saw Billy the Kid pick up the knife belonging to his mother, Celsa Gutierrez, from their home the night he was killed.

Frederick Nolan came into possession of the knife after convincing Maxwell descendants in Tennessee to sell it to him. After Nolan, the knife found its way to the Robert McCubbin collection before it was auctioned off in 2019 for $118,000.

Nolan, Frederick. "The Saga of the Kid's Butcher Knife". 1997.

The funeral of Billy the Kid. *Illustration by Larry Gosser.*

INQUEST AND BURIAL

Within a very short time after the shooting, quite a number of the native people had gathered around, some of them bewailing the death of their friend, while several women pleaded for permission to take charge of the body, which we allowed them to do. They carried it across the yard to a carpenter shop, where it was laid out on a work-bench, the women placing lighted candles around it according to their ideas of properly conducting a 'wake' for the dead.

> One of the most controversial aspects of that night was the immediate placement of Billy's body following his death. Poe maintains that the body was allowed to be removed to the nearby carpenter's shop. Garrett remains somewhat vague and only states that the inquest was held the following morning. Jesus Silva corroborates Poe's statement but credits Pete Maxwell with the idea of moving Billy's body. Silva states, "We asked permission to remove the body, Pete Maxwell suggested removal to the old carpenter's shop." In the same interview, he goes on to say, "A few moments later I returned to the room, picked up the lifeless body of Billy and walked into a large hallway in the Maxwell home, laid his body on a long table. I there examined him again and ascertained without doubt he was dead. The body was then

removed to an old carpenter shop nearby where Billy was laid out."

The conflict arises when considering Paco Anaya's later interview, in which he claims, "I went to Segudo's house, got him, and the jury of above-named men was sworn in. We viewed Billy's body at the Maxwell home." This statement suggests that the body was viewed by the jury before being moved to the carpenter's shop, as Poe claimed. Paco also mentions that there were two coroner's reports, the first of which was misplaced. This would account for the initial viewing. The second report, which Milnor Rudulph presided over, occurred the following morning after the killing and states that it took place in the Maxwell home. This aligns with the time it would have taken Rudulph to ride into Fort Sumner from Sunnyside.

Upon closer examination of the details surrounding the coroner's report, the conflict primarily derives from the accounts of Paco Anaya and Milnor Rudulph. Both accounts are taken from their personal memoirs and interviews conducted years after the event. It is worth noting that Paco is the only person to refer to a previous coroner's report that was lost or discarded. Moreover, Paco Anaya's name does not appear in any other sources, while Rudulph's involvement is confirmed as his name appears on the coroner's report. This raises the question of whether Paco Anaya was intricately involved in the death and burial of Billy the Kid, as he claimed.

Source:
Los Bilitos, *pp. 251-252*
I Buried Billy, *pp. 128-132*
Clovis News Journal, *Tuesday, July 26, 1938*

All that occurred after the Kid came into view in the yard, up to the time he was killed, happened in much less time than it takes to tell it, not more than thirty seconds

THE DEATH OF BILLY THE KID: ANNOTATED EDITION

intervening between the time I first saw him and the time he was shot. From Garrett's statement of what took place in the room after he entered, it appears that he left his Winchester rifle standing by the side of the door, and approached the bed where Maxwell was sleeping, arousing him and sitting down on the edge of the bed near the head.

A moment after he had taken this position for a talk with Maxwell, he heard voices on the porch and sat quietly listening, when a man appeared in the doorway and a moment later ran up to Maxwell's bed, saying, 'Pete, who are those fellows outside?' It being dark in the room, he had not up to the moment seen Garrett sitting at the head of the bed.

When he spoke to Maxwell, Garrett recognized his voice and made a move to draw his six-shooter. This movement attracted the Kid's attention, and, seeing that a man was sitting there, he instantly covered him with his gun, backed away, and demanded several times in Spanish to know who it was. Garrett made no reply, and, without rising from his seat, fired with the result stated.

The most accepted time for the killing of Billy the Kid is just a few minutes before midnight on July 14th. However, the account given by Pvt. George Miller provides us with a different timeframe. Pvt. Miller was a recently discharged Buffalo Soldier out of Fort Stanton. Miller advised that he was awakened at 12:30 in the morning to the sound of gunshots. He witnessed the Kid's body after going to the Maxwell residence to look into the cause of the commotion. Miller also helped dig the Kid's grave and was present at the Kid's funeral that afternoon. Pvt. Miller left Fort Sumner and arrived in Las Vegas on the 17th, reporting his account of the events to a reporter at the Las Vegas Daily Optic.

John W. Poe and Josh W. Slatten

Source: Las Vegas Daily Optic, *Las Vegas, New Mexico, July 18, 1881, p.4*

Private George Miller. Unknown date. *Photo courtesy of Ancestry.*

This occurred at about midnight on the fourteenth of July 1881. We spent the remainder of the night on the Maxwell premises, keeping constantly on our guard, as we were expecting to be attacked by the friends of the dead man. Nothing of the kind occurred, however...

Sophie Poe provides much more detail about her husband's interactions with John Jacobs on the night in question. She writes: "As the body was carried out of Maxwell's, Jacobs came running, out of breath, carrying his gun. He saw John William and relaxed. 'I was falling asleep when I heard the shots. I was afraid I wouldn't see you alive, but I grabbed up my gun and came running.'" Sophia continues, "It was typical, not merely of John Jacobs, but of frontier friendship. The idea of finding himself in a fight with all of Fort Sumner had not deterred Jacobs for an instant—not when a friend of his might be in danger." She goes on to suggest that Jacobs may have joined the three lawmen as they fortified themselves inside the Maxwell residence, anticipating a possible confrontation with the locals.

If Sophie's account is accurate, it introduces the possibility that another individual, John Jacobs, witnessed the death of Billy the Kid and the events of that night.
Source: Buckboard Days, *p.116.*

...the next morning, we sent for a justice of the peace, who held an inquest over the body, the verdict of the jury being such as to justify the killing.

The report was initially handed over by Pat Garrett to District Attorney William Breeden of the First Judicial District following the Kid's death. It was filed with the San Miguel County court records and discovered in 1932 by Harold Abbott, a State Land Office employee, in the Capitol Building's basement. This significant find was mentioned in Frank M. King's 1935 book, Wrangling the Past: Reminiscences of Frank King. *King references Garrett's July 15th letter to Acting Governor Ritch, which cited the existence of the coroner's report.*

Another noteworthy mention of the report appears on the front page of the Alamogordo News *(November 30, 1950), in an article titled "Sumner Jury Thought the Kid Had Been Killed." The article states, "He, with other employees, were going over some old records in the basement of the state capital. There they ran across, in the San Miguel Court records, the original copy of the coroner's jury, dated July 15, 1881, and written in Spanish."*

Unfortunately, the coroner's report has once again been lost, or it may reside in a private collection. Fortunately for historians, copies were made before it disappeared. Like the

Kid himself, these papers have proven elusive, continuing to intrigue those who seek the truth behind Billy the Kid's final moments.

Source: Cooper, Gale. The Coroner's Jury of Billy the Kid. Gelcour Books, 2019, pp. 43-45.

William G. Ritch. Acting Governor of the New Mexico Territory.

Later on the same day, the body was buried in the old military burying ground at Fort Sumner.

> There are several accounts of Billy the Kid's funeral, though some appear more suspect than others. One of the more questionable accounts comes from a Texas cowboy named Jack Potter, who moved to Fort Sumner in 1884, just three years after the Kid's death. Potter recounted many firsthand stories he had heard, as the topic still lingered in local conversation. In his detailed version, Potter claims that Garrett instructed the locals to construct a crude coffin from the roof planks of a nearby adobe structure. Once finished, the lifeless body was placed inside the makeshift coffin and

The Death of Billy the Kid: Annotated Edition

carried to the cemetery, located just east of the spot where Billy was killed.

Late in the afternoon of July 15, 1881, Billy the Kid's funeral supposedly took place. According to Potter's story, every resident of Fort Sumner, including the saloon keeper, attended—an event so significant that the saloon closed its doors for the only time anyone could remember. The service was said to have referred to Billy as "our beloved young citizen," a phrase that, if true, indicates the affection and respect many in the area held for him. A passage from the Book of Job was read: "A man that is born of a woman is of few days and full of trouble—he fleeth like a shadow and continueth not." The service concluded with the words, "Billy cannot come back to us, but we can go to him and will see him again up yonder, Amen." Potter also mentions that the day after the funeral, Pete Maxwell had his men create a crude wooden marker by sawing off pieces of the parade-ground fence, assembling them into a cross, and painting "BILLY THE KID, JULY 14, 1881" in rough letters.

Paulita Jaramillo (Maxwell) offers a similar remembrance of the funeral. She recalls that Francisco Medina knocked together a coffin out of rough pine boards, and the hearse was nothing more than an old, creaking wagon drawn by scrawny ponies. She states that virtually the entire population of the town followed the body to the small cemetery. "You might have thought the funeral that of Fort Sumner's most distinguished citizen," she said. Billy was buried next to Charlie Bowdre and Tom Folliard—Folliard's grave at one end, Bowdre's in the middle, and Billy's at the other end. Paulita also recalls a wooden cross placed at the head of Billy's grave, painted with his name in crude, zigzagging letters.

A third notable account comes from Jesus Silva. In an interview with the Clovis News, Silva stated, "The next *morning at 10 o'clock we buried Billy the Kid in the little cemetery near the old Fort, beside the bodies of Billy's former pals, Charlie Bowdre and Tom O'Falliard, who were killed by officers earlier. I was chief pallbearer at Billy's funeral that morning. With me were Antonio Savedera, Saval Guttierez, Vicente Otero, and a few others. We buried The Kid in a grave which had been dug by Vicente Otero."*

While details vary between these accounts, their common threads—an improvised coffin, the communal attendance, burial next to Bowdre and Folliard, and the makeshift grave marker—suggest a sincere, if simple, tribute from the people of Fort Sumner. Together, these narratives offer valuable insights into the final farewell given to one of the most storied outlaws of the American West.

Source:

Burns, Walter Noble. *"The Belle of Old Fort Sumner."* University of Arizona.

Burroughs, Jean. On the Trail. *Museum of New Mexico Press.*

Duplicate of the Kid's original marker.

Fort Sumner. The viewer is looking west towards the Maxwell home. The Gutierrez home is in the row of adobes that occupies the center of this image and shows the route that Billy the Kid is believed to have taken on the night of July 14, 1881, just before being shot in the bedroom of Pete Maxwell.

There have been many wild and untrue stories of this affair, one of which was that we had in some way learned in advance that the Kid would come to Maxwell's residence that night, and had concealed ourselves there with the purpose of waylaying and killing him. Another was that we had cut off fingers and carried them away as trophies or souvenirs, and in later years it has been said many times that the Kid was not dead at all but had been seen alive and well in various places.

Multiple newspapers at the time published sensational claims that Billy the Kid's body parts were turning up as curiosities. One such report appeared in The Las Vegas Daily Optic *on July 25, 1881:*

"THE FAT FINGER. An esteemed friend of The Optic *at Fort Sumner, L. W. Hale, has sent us the index finger of 'Billy the Kid,' the one which has snapped many a*

man's life into eternity. It is well preserved in alcohol and has been viewed by many in our office today. If the rush continues we shall purchase a small tent and open a sideshow, to which complimentary tickets will be issued to our personal friends."

Another account appeared in the Albuquerque Journal on October 31, 1885:

"Jim Carlin, who lives in the old curiosity shop, is now engaged in extensive correspondence attempting to prove that the miserable little misshapen death head in his possession is really and truly the skull of Billy the Kid, the talented young murderer and cattle thief, who made considerable reputation in this territory at one time and was finally put to sleep by Pat Garrett. The skull was presented to Col. J. G. Albright, on his recent visit to Santa Fe, by Mr. Harlow, the fat landlord, and Mr. Albright presented it to Mr. Carlin. Mr. Harlow says that Pat Garrett presented the skull to him, and solemnly assured him that it was an authentic piece of bone, and had formerly contained the very limited quantity of brains the good Lord had doled out to Billy the Kid."

Charles Siringo specifically addresses the claim about Billy the Kid's trigger finger supposedly being preserved in a jar of alcohol. According to Siringo, Garrett returned to Fort Sumner and exhumed the Kid's body, confirming that the trigger finger remained attached to his right hand. While this may seem far-fetched, Garrett himself later refuted any claims that the Kid's remains had been disturbed or displayed. In The Authentic Life of Billy the Kid, he states, "Again I say that the Kid's body lies undisturbed in the grave—and I speak of what I know."

Source:
History of Billy the Kid, p.133
Authentic Life, p.178

The Death of Billy the Kid: Annotated Edition

"This is the Place," He Said—Where Billy the Kid was Shot

Photo in the *Saturday Evening Post* from about 1904 when Pat Garrett, above, returned to the Kid's grave.

The actual facts, however, are exactly as stated herein, and while we no doubt would, under the circumstances, have lain in wait for him at the Maxwell premises if there had been the slightest reason for believing that he would come there, the fact that he did come was a complete surprise to us, absolutely unexpected and unlooked for as far as we three were concerned. The story that we had cut off and carried away his fingers was even more absurd, as the thought of such a thing never entered our minds, and besides, we were not that kind of people.

Nearly a century and a half has passed since Billy the Kid's death. In that time, numerous charlatans have stepped forward, each claiming to be the Kid. While these assertions may help sustain the outlaw's legend, they serve little purpose beyond enriching those who peddle these fictions. Their claims, therefore, merit no more attention than the few sentences already allotted to them.

The grave of Billy the Kid. Photo taken in 2024.

The killing of the Kid created a great sensation throughout the South-west, and many of the law-abiding citizens of New Mexico and the Panhandle contributed substantially and liberally toward a reward for the officers whose work had finally rid the country of a man who was nothing less than a scourge.

The day after Garrett killed Billy the Kid, he composed a letter addressed to Acting-Governor William Ritch. Enclosed with the letter was a copy of the Coroner's Jury report, providing details surrounding Billy the Kid's death. The contents of this letter were quoted in the July 23, 1881,

The Death of Billy the Kid: Annotated Edition

publication of the Las Cruces Rio Grand Republican. The article bore the title, "Kid the Killer Killed: Wm. Bonney alias Antrim, alias Billy the Kid, Fatally Meets Pat Garrett, the Lincoln County Sheriff."

Sheriff Garrett met with Governor Ritch on July 20, 1881, a meeting documented by the Santa Fe Daily New Mexican. *Governor Ritch expressed his willingness to pay the amount promised but explained that he needed to review the records first. Since he had not been present in the city when the offer was made and had received no prior notification, he was unsure if the reward had been officially documented. In essence, Governor Lew Wallace had failed to file the necessary paperwork to reinstate the reward on Billy the Kid after his escape from Lincoln.*

As a result of this administrative oversight, the offer lacked official state recognition and had to be brought before the legislature. On February 18, 1882, the legislature granted Garrett the $500 reward. During the session, it was mentioned that the reward had initially been refused on a "technicality." Between this legislative reward and the donations made by private donors, Garrett ultimately received a total of $7,000—equivalent to more than $220,000 in today's dollars—for killing Billy the Kid.

Source:
Trial, *pp. 183–184.*

The taking-off of the Kid had a very salutary effect in New Mexico and the Panhandle, most of his followers leaving the country, for the time being at least, and a great many persons who had sympathized with him or been terrorized by him completely changed their attitude toward the enforcement of law.

The events which occurred at Maxwell's ranch on the night of that fourteenth of July to this day seem to me strange and mysterious, as the Kid was certainly a 'killer,' was absolutely desperate, and had the drop first on me and then on Garrett. Why did he not use it? Possibly because he thought he was in the house of his friends and had no suspicion that the officers of the law would ever come to that place searching for him. From what we learned afterward, there was some reason for believing that we had been seen leaving the peach orchard by one of his friends, who ran to the house where he was stopping for the night, warning him of our presence. Upon which he had run out half-dressed to Maxwell's, thinking that, by reason of the standing of the Maxwell family, he would not be sought there. However this may be, it is still, in view of his character and the condition he was in, a mystery.

I have been in many close places and through many trying experiences both before and after this occurrence, but never in one where I was so forcibly impressed with the idea that a Higher Power controls and rules the destinies of men. To me it seemed that what occurred in Fort Sumner that night had actually been foreordained.

The foregoing sketch or narrative was written at odd moments, taken from a very busy business life, upon the urgent request and oft-repeated solicitations of friends, and it is the first —and probably the last — attempt of the writer to record any of the facts related.

This is one of the few instances in which Poe discusses the events surrounding Billy the Kid's death. While killing Billy the Kid defined Garrett's legacy, Poe's involvement appears to be little more than a footnote in what most would consider a successful and accomplished life.

The Final Moments of Billy the Kid
A Pictorial Essay

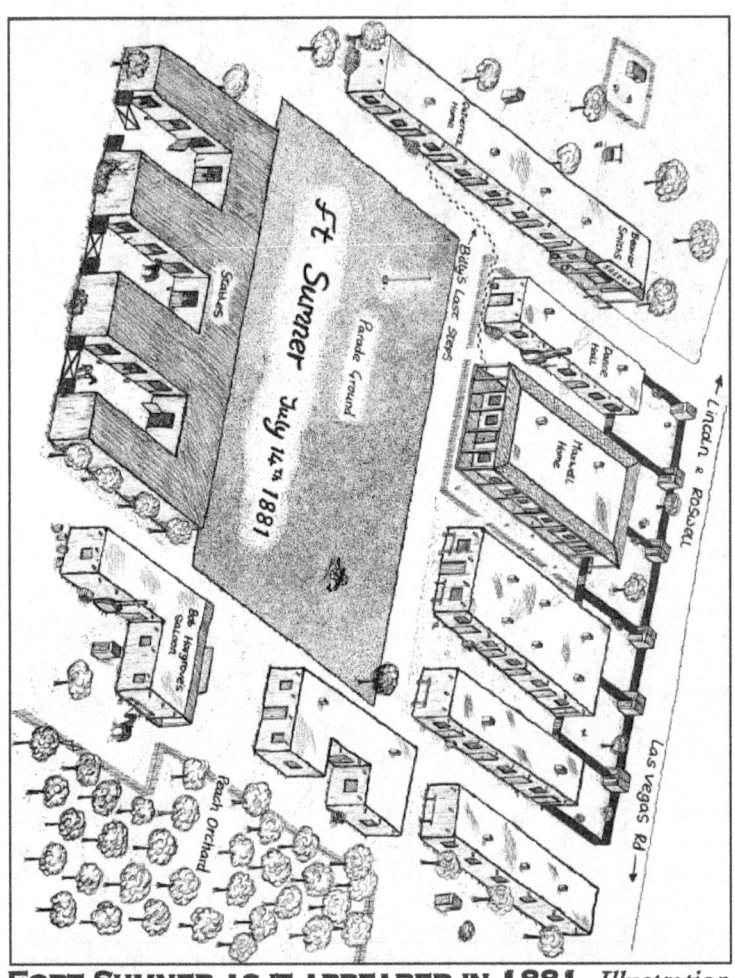

Fort Sumner as it appeared in 1881 *Illustration by Mel Hubner.*

BILLY THE KID'S PERSPECTIVE *Illustration by Mel Hubner.*

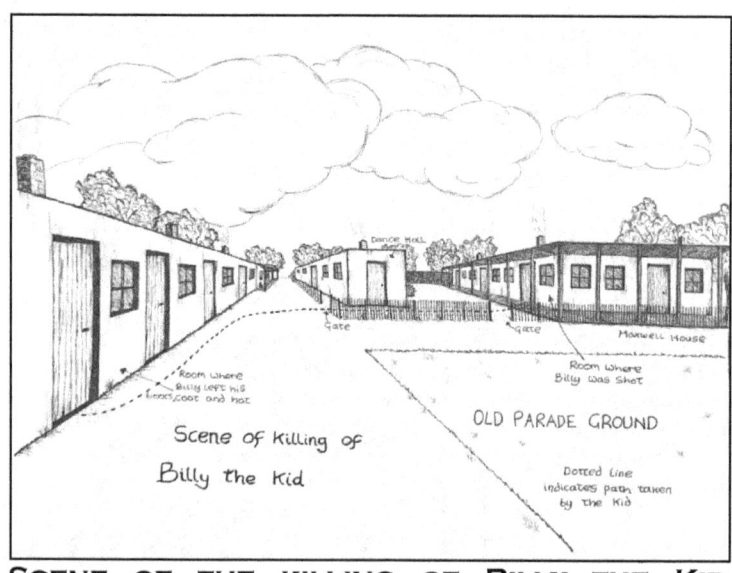

SCENE OF THE KILLING OF BILLY THE KID *Illustration by Mel Hubner.* This is a revision taken from illustration that appeared in the original text. The roof was drawn to show the Maxwell residence as a flat roofed adobe as described by Poe.

BILLY THE KID'S DEATH SITE Placed in 2024, the recently erected monument marks the location where Billy the Kid was killed. This location was originally off limits to the general public and was marked by a simple pile of bricks.

SITE OF THE MAXWELL HOME 2024 The viewer is looking west towards what would have been the front porch of the Maxwell home. The location of Beaver Smith's Saloon can be seen to the left of the monument, approximately 75 yards in the distance. It's at Beaver's that witnesses claim the wake was held and the entire town paid their respects to their fallen friend.

THE PEACH ORCHARD The three lawmen maintained a watchful eye on the town of Fort Sumner from the peach orchard which was located on the north side of the fort, less than 100 yards from the Maxwell Residence. The viewer is looking north from what was once the parade ground toward the location where the orchard once stood.

The Death of Billy the Kid: Annotated Edition

BILLY'S LAST WALK Just minutes before his death, Billy walked from the Gutierrez home to the bedroom of Pete Maxwell. The photograph is taken from the position of the Pete's bedroom, looking east towards the location of the Gutierrez home. The center tree indicates the original location of the home, prior to the Pecos River flooding and altering the terrain.

THE PARADE GROUNDS The viewer is looking north east from the general location of the Maxwell Residence home site.

THE CARPENTERS SHOP After Billy's body was removed from the Maxwell Residence, it was relocated to the carpenter's shop, located at the far east of side of the village. The current walkway marks the route his slain body traveled in preparation for his wake and burial that came the following day. The location of the original carpenter's shop stood near the current location of the Bosque Redondo Memorial.

THE VILLAGE OF FORT SUMNER An overhead view of what was once the Village of Fort Sumner. The newly placed stone marker, indicating the location where Billy the Kid's body fell dead, can be seen on the right side of the image

The last image taken of John Poe, shortly before his death in 1923. *Courtesy of the Historical Society for Southeast New Mexico.*

The Death
of John W. Poe

While Poe is often remembered primarily as the deputy who aided in killing Billy the Kid, his life encompassed far more than that single event. After leaving law enforcement, he became a world traveler and renowned businessman. Poe helped organize the Bank of Roswell, serving as its first president from 1893 to 1899, before helping establish the Citizens Bank of Roswell. This new venture thrived, and the bank was nationalized in 1903.

John Poe amassed substantial wealth through his various business enterprises, enabling him to take his beloved Sophia on a leisurely trip around the world in 1913. The two were inseparable, each serving as the other's foundation during their golden years.

Poe remained active and enjoyed good health until his final days. He was known by all as an ethical, honest man who placed Sophia's well-being, as well as that of others, above his own. He showed kindness to everyone he encountered and abhorred violence unless all other options had been exhausted.

JOHN W. POE AND JOSH W. SLATTEN

John and Sophie Poe and the home that John built for his beloved Sophie. The home still stands in Roswell's Downtown Historic District. *Both courtesy Historical Society for Southeast New Mexico.*

The Death of Billy the Kid: Annotated Edition

John William Poe drew his last breaths at the Battle Creek Sanitarium in Michigan on July 27, 1923, at 9 p.m. His death might surprise those familiar with the numerous dangers he had faced—surviving rough pioneer towns like Fort Bivins and Mobeetie, and confronting Billy the Kid himself. Yet Poe did not die "with his boots on," like so many hard characters of his era. Instead, he passed away in bed, succumbing to pneumonia after only a few short days of illness. His health declined so rapidly that Sophia, who was visiting Chicago, was en route to Michigan at the time of his death. His body was transported back to Roswell, where he was laid to rest.

Some previous historians have erroneously claimed his death was a suicide, though no source supporting this fictional narrative has ever been found. Poe's bout with pneumonia was brief and unexpected, leading swiftly to his untimely passing.

The news of his death was met with great sorrow in Roswell, where his influence on the community had endured for more than four decades. Today, John William Poe rests peacefully in South Park Cemetery alongside his beloved Sophia and their infant son, who died during childbirth. May they continue to rest in eternal peace.

"John Poe filled a big place in the life of Roswell and the Pecos Valley and in every way will be missed."

—*Roswell Daily Record*, July 18, 1923

Source:
Albuquerque Journal, July 19, 1923.
Roswell Daily Record, July 18, 1923.
Buckboard Days, pp. 265–268.

The final resting place of John and Sophie Poe. (South Park Cemetery, Roswell, NM, 2021.)

Epilogue

When I embarked on the journey to re-release this book, I originally envisioned a substantial distinction between the narratives of John Poe and Pat Garrett. Yet, as you proceed through these pages, even with over fifty additional annotations, you will see that there is, in fact, minimal disparity between the two men's accounts of the hunt, death, and burial of Billy the Kid. Are there differences in their stories? Certainly. When dealing with two Type-A personalities like Poe and Garrett, small discrepancies are to be expected.

The primary distinctions that arise when comparing their accounts stem from each man's desire to be viewed as the "hero." Poe's version strongly implies that he initiated their trip to Fort Sumner and the decision to speak with Maxwell. In contrast, Garrett suggests he orchestrated the events. Both men were pursuing their own objectives, and the differences in their stories may have been unintentional rather than deliberate attempts to mislead.

The details surrounding the events of July 14, 1881, become even more obscure when we consider the accounts of bystanders. While the narratives provided by Jesus Silva and Frank Lobato appear to complement each other, they differ from Paco Anaya's chronology.

Furthermore, depending on the storyteller, Deluvina Maxwell's role in that night's proceedings shifts. In one version, she plays a part during the night's events; in another, she isn't even in town until the next morning.

Whether you believe John Poe or Pat Garrett took the lead that night has little bearing on the outcome. Billy the Kid undoubtedly met his end on a hot summer evening in Pete Maxwell's bedroom. His body was cared for, clothed, and mourned by those who knew him before being buried in the place he had chosen as his sanctuary. Having fled Lincoln with two dead deputies behind him, Billy found something in Fort Sumner that made it feel like home. Beyond fear of capture or death, he claimed this place as his own. It is fitting that he rests in the very ground he turned to in adversity. We should all be so fortunate.

While the specifics of that night may never be fully understood, one fact remains certain: Pat Garrett never escaped the shadow of that event. Misfortune followed him until the end, and the killing of Billy the Kid defined his public persona. John Poe, on the other hand, moved beyond that night to create a life that exceeded even the boldest expectations of his era. With a law enforcement career beyond reproach, successful business ventures, and global travels, Poe proved that his legacy encompassed far more than a single fateful evening.

Like Billy, Poe lived life on his own terms. Perhaps the lawman and the young bandit shared more in common than it initially appears.

INDEX

Anaya, Paco, 56, 59, 73, 92, 102-103, 105, 108, 133
Authentic Life of Billy the Kid, The, 49, 51-53, 82, 84-85, 94, 96, 98-99, 116
Beaver Smith's Saloon, 71, 124
Bell, J.W., 33, 50, 53
Bernstein, Morris, 17
Bonney, C.D., 68
Bosque Redondo, 15, 126
Bowdre, Charlie, 31-32, 113-114
Brady, Sheriff William, 15, 18, 29
Brent, James, 46
Brininstool, E.A., 37
Bristol, Warren, 30, 33
Burns, Walter Noble, 40, 52, 89
Campbell, Tom, 18
Capitan Mountains, 54
Carlyle, James, 22, 32
Cattlemen's Association, 14
Chapman, Huston J., 19-20, 27-29
Chisum, John S., 30
Cline, Donald, 92-93

Coghlan, Pat, 20, 31, 42, 56
Collins, John, 72-73
Dedrick, Sam, 59
Dolan, James J., 18-19, 27, 29-30
Dudley, Colonel Nathan, 19
Elk, NM, 54
Evans, Jesse, 18-19, 29
Folliard, Tom, 16, 18, 20, 31-32, 113-114
Fort Griffin, TX, 12-13
Fort Stanton, NM, 19-20, 27, 51, 109
Fort Sumner, NM, 15-17, 30-32, 35, 40, 54, 59, 61-84, 91, 94, 98, 108-116, 120-121, 124, 127, 133-134
Fulton, Maurice, 9, 11, 38, 53, 72
Garrett, Apolinaria, 91
Garrett, Sheriff Patrick F., 32-33, 36, 43, 46-49, 51-53, 56-58, 61-63, 65-67, 69, 72-73, 75-78, 81-88, 91-92, 94-96, 98-104, 107, 109, 111-112, 116-120, 133-134

Goodnight, Charles, 37, 41
Grant, Joe, 71
Greathouse Ranch, 32
Gutierrez, Celsa, 87, 92, 105, 115
Hindman, George, 15, 18, 29
I Buried Billy, 56, 73, 74
Jacobs, John Cloud, 82
Kimbrell, Sheriff George, 29
La Mesilla, NM, 29, 33-34
Las Cruces, NM, 61, 119
Las Portales Lake, 31
Las Tablas, NM, 20, 27, 48-49, 54
Lea, Captain J.C., 36, 68
Lea, J.S., 65
Lea-Bonney Company Store, 67-68
Lincoln County War, 14, 17, 27, 31, 53
Lincoln, NM, 14-19, 27, 29, 31-33, 43, 45, 48-49, 51, 53-54, 57, 59-61, 65-67, 77, 92, 99, 119, 134
Lobato, Frank, 133
"Los Bilitos": The Story of 'Billy the Kid' And His Gang, 76-77, 99, 108

Maxwell home, 35, 85-86, 90, 103, 107-108, 115, 124
Maxwell Land Grant, 16
Maxwell, Deluvina, 16, 100-101, 103-105, 134
Maxwell, Lucien B., 16, 86
Maxwell, Paulita, 17, 40, 63, 87, 90, 105, 113
Maxwell, Pete, 16, 36, 62-63, 77, 81, 84-85, 87-88, 90, 94-95, 98-102, 107, 109, 113, 115, 125, 134
McKinney, Cliff, 62
McKinney, Kip, 62, 64-67, 84-86, 90, 93
McSween, Susan, 19
Meadows, John B., 54, 56, 59
Mesilla, NM, 41, 60-61, 63
Metz, Leon, 62
Miller, George, 109-110
Mullin, Robert N., 87
Nolan, Frederick, 104-105
Olinger, Robert, 33-34, 50-52
Otero, Vicente, 114
Patron Store, 29
Pickett, Tom, 22, 31-32

Poe, John W.
  as buffalo hunter, 12
  as Deputy United
    States Marshal, 13
  as Mason, 57
  death of, 131
  early life of, 12
  gun of, 80
  in White Oaks, 43-45
  meeting Pat Garrett,
    43
  on the burial of the
    Kid, 107-120
  on the night of July
    14, 1881, 81-105
  personal life and later
    years, 129
  trailing the Kid, 51-
    79
  writing of *The Death
    of Billy the Kid*, 37
Poe, Sophie, 47, 53, 57,
  62, 110-111
Potter, Jack, 101-102,
  112
Powers, Tom, 91
Ringo, Johnny, 48, 76
Ritch, William G., 112,
  118
Roswell, NM, 11-12,
  36, 64-68, 129, 131
Rudabaugh, Dave, 31,
  32, 91
Rudulph, Charles, 78

Rudulph, Milnor, 48,
  75-76, 78-79, 108
Rynerson, William L.,
  30
Saga of Billy the Kid, The,
  52-53
Salazar, Yginio, 20, 54-
  55
Santa Fe jail, 25, 33, 41
Santa Fe, NM, 12, 25,
  29, 33-34, 41, 86,
  116, 119
Seymour, Edward, 37
Silva, Jesus, 83-84, 107,
  113, 133
Siringo, Charles, 88, 92-
  93, 116
Smith, Beaver, 69
Stewart, Frank, 31-32
Stinking Springs, NM,
  32, 91
Sunnyside, NM, 75, 108
Tascosa, TX, 31
Texas Panhandle, 11,
  13, 42, 45
Thomas, David, 26, 57
Tombstone, AZ, 48, 76
Tularosa, NM, 31, 42,
  56, 61
Tunstall Store, 15
Wallace, Governor
  Lew, 17-18, 20, 27,
  30, 43, 119

White Oaks, NM, 32, 42-48, 51, 57-64, 66, 71
Wide World Magazine, 35, 37
Wilson, Billy, 31-32, 59, 91
Wilson, Squire J.B., 21
Yerby Ranch, 73-74

About the Author

Josh Slatten is the Executive Director of Billy the Kid's Historical Coalition, where he channels his lifelong passion for Billy the Kid. A prolific researcher and author, Josh has written a best-selling children's book about Billy the Kid and has contributed to numerous historical magazines, journals, and books. Josh is a career police officer and has been married to his beautiful wife, Britt for twenty years. With his free time, he enjoys the company of his two best friends, his French Bulldogs, Molly and Josie.

www.ingramcontent.com/pod-product-compliance
Lightning Source LLC
Chambersburg PA
CBHW050256010526
44107CB00033B/1396/J